7 Steps to Effective Communication

GOODWILL PUBLISHING HOUSE®
B-3 RATTAN JYOTI, 18 RAJENDRA PLACE
NEW DELHI-110008 (INDIA)

Published by
GOODWILL PUBLISHING HOUSE®
B-3 Rattan Jyoti, 18 Rajendra Place
New Delhi-110008 (INDIA)
Tel. : 25750801, 25820556
Fax : 91-11-25764396
E-mail : goodwillpub@vsnl.net
website : www.goodwillpublishinghouse.com

Printed at Kumar Offset Printers, Delhi-110092

Contents

Preface

An interpersonal relationship is built upon an individual's ability to communicate effectively with another individual. Using the faculty of speech, mankind has evolved almost 5,000 languages and dialects as a medium to communicate with each other. Written form of languages emerged from the need to record oral communication. However, communication is not restricted to spoken or written words. Body language communicates much more than one would imagine.

Communication amongst people fails because individuals are pre-occupied with personal problems and thoughts. Because of these pre-occupations people fail to be receptive to what they hear or read. Most people fail to interpret the body language correctly.

Everybody does not look at the same thing in the same way. There are vast variations because of individual background and opinion. This further aggravates the problem of effective communication.

The solution lies in a person's ability to perceive spoken, written and body languages correctly. This is possible only when a person breaks the self-created barrier of pre-occupation, and concentrates on what one hears, reads or observes. Only the person who listens correctly can respond effectively. Only the person who reads and understands correctly can write effectively. Only the person who observes body signals and interprets them correctly can maintain self-restraint.

This book aims at taking you step by step into the intricacies of listening, speaking, writing and observing body language. It helps you to carry out self-assessment of your strengths and weaknesses in life, and in using the information for enhancing your strengths and overcoming your limitations. Through determination and perseverance, you can develop skills and abilities to communicate effectively.

— Prem P. Bhalla

You are Always Communicating

Every individual comes to this world alone. Even twins, triplets and quadruplets are born one by one, one coming after the other. After living for years, months and days, as destined, every individual leaves this world alone. However, in the period from birth to death, every individual makes many kinds of relationships, each requiring communication to keep the relationship alive and beneficial.

The need for communication is not restricted only to human beings. It is equally important to plant and animal life. Since our interest in the subject aims at learning to understand how communication works amongst human beings, and how every individual can make his or her life more effective by understanding the various factors involved, we will restrict the present study to human beings, as we go step by step to learn how to communicate better.

At the very outset, we must understand that communication plays a very important role in everyone's life. We communicate in many ways. Some ways are immediately understood, but many times we communicate even without being aware of it. The truth is that we are always communicating. Unbelievable? You will understand this better as we go deeper into the subject.

UNDERSTANDING COMMUNICATION

Communication is an act or process of sharing or exchanging of thoughts, opinions or information. It also refers to something imparted, interchanged or transmitted. In general, it refers to the use of speech or written words, as is done through verbal or written messages from person to person, as on telephone, or through facsimile machine or post.

In wider sense, communication also refers to passing on an emotion, disease or heat. We often hear of people conveying their feelings not through vocal or written messages, but by their sheer presence. We also hear of communicable diseases, and the need to guard against them. Scientists will tell you of heat passing quickly through some metals, and slowly through others. Human emotions are equally responsive to communication, being sensitive to both the positive and negative forms. Sharing of intimate thoughts and feelings influence all human beings.

It would be wrong to restrict communication only to spoken or written words. Much is communicated even through silence, when one uses it as a tool to introspect, or talk to oneself. We have also seen how silence is used to punish another person by not talking to him or her. This is a common sight amongst couples, or children and parents. Even friends go into the silent mode occasionally to settle personal scores.

Have you noticed how people communicate through their actions; through their clothes, and even makeup? Women spend much time in dressing and makeup to communicate that they are beautiful. Some decorate their hair with flowers. It is common for both men and women to wear perfumes that convey different kinds of messages.

We have all seen and heard a radio. A distant voice comes through space and reaches us through the radio. In the same way, sound and images are transmitted to television sets via satellites. Science has made it possible to communicate in many ways.

People of different religions and faiths go to different places of worship like a temple, a mosque, a church not only to pray or pay obeisance to a deity, but also for the great pleasure and peace they experience in these places. This experience was not easy to explain earlier. However, now everyone agrees that positive vibrations abound in these places, and under their influence, one feels the tranquility and peace. Positive feelings generate positive vibrations. These are communicated in silence.

Think it over...

Facts are God's arguments; we should be careful never to misunderstand or pervert them.

— *Tryon Edwards*

COMMUNICATION AND ANIMALS

Although we will restrict this study to communication between human beings, it would be useful to understand that although animals do not understand the various languages human beings speak all over the world, they respond to what they are taught. In their own way they communicate with human beings. If it were not for this, we would not have had millions of pet lovers all over the world. Dogs and cats are the most popular pets. Everyone has seen how pets react to love, scolding or care. Birds also are good pets. In the era gone by, pigeons were trained to carry messages. Parrots are known to copy human speech.

It is again due to effective communication that it has been possible to use animals for the welfare of mankind. Dogs have a developed sense of smell. Trained sniffing squads are used to trace drugs, bombs and explosives. They also help trace criminals. In the cold snowy regions, they are also known to pull sledges and trace people lost in blizzards.

Elephants, camels, yak, horses, bullocks and mules carry loads and pull ploughs and implements to make land yield larger quantities of grain. The milch animals, particularly cow is known to respond very well to human communication.

If it were not for communication skills it might not have been possible to see the many animals perform interesting tricks in a circus. Even the wild animals have been trained to perform. Dolphins are friendly and are a part of every sea resort where they perform. Tamed bears and monkeys dance to the tune of their masters in many Indian streets. Snake charmers are also commonly seen.

The initial lessons taught to children pertain to stories of animals. Even grownups find stories about animals interesting and educative. In the Ramayan, we read about bears, monkeys, squirrels and even the vulture coming to support Sri Ram in his battle to get Sita back. In the Mahabharat, we read of Yudhistra leading a dog to heaven. 'The Panchtantra' is a great collection of educational stories in which animals feature just like human beings. Aesop's Fables are equally important to teach human values. The modern child is also acquainted with animal characters that form a part of comic strips and interesting films.

If animals can respond to communication techniques, it is obvious that all living beings instinctively respond to different kinds of communication. The important lesson for all of us is that through understanding and training, it is possible to learn good communication skills.

COMMUNICATION AND PLANTS

Although it is only of academic importance to the average person, but in their own way plants also communicate within themselves, and also with the non-plant organisms, particularly in the root region. Nitrogen fixing bacteria are attracted to the roots of the leguminous plants, and help increase soil productivity. Vegetable products that grow within the soil are known to respond to the bacteria and fungi in the soil. Some plants are carnivorous. Most of them are not. When attacked by insects they produce volatile substances that attract parasites capable of putting an end to the insects.

Flowers attract through their vibrant colours and fragrance. The insects that are attracted help the process of pollination and continuity of the species. The honeybee finds honey in the nectar of the flowers. It is interesting to note that the medicinal qualities of plants have been known since time immemorial, and form a part of the study of Ayurveda. Hindus are also known to respect several plants as sacred, the most important ones being the Peepal tree and the Tulsi plant. Tulsi plant can be seen growing in the courtyard of many Hindu homes. Many Hindus worship it everyday.

> **Think it over...**
>
> How far that little candle throws its beams:
> So shines a good deed in a naughty world.
>
> — *Sh* *peare*

COMMUNICATION BEGINS EARLY

Few look at it that way, but messages are sent out and reach us in strange ways. Have you seen how a woman reacts when she gets to know that she is going to become a mother? The unborn child cannot speak or write, but has already communicated that a baby will arrive in due time. The father and others soon get to know about it, and each reacts in different ways.

As the unborn baby grows, it is believed that the mother and the child can communicate with each other. The mother can feel the baby growing. The bonds between the two grow, and gradually become a source of love and attachment.

Hindus believe that the thoughts and actions of the mother influence the unborn baby. In the Mahabharat, there is the mention of Arjun's son Abhimanyu, who learnt the art of warfare in his mother's womb. In the Bhagwat Puran, there is the mention of Bhakta Prahlad's mother Kyadhu listening to sermons narrated by Narad, influencing the unborn Prahlad. Sukhdev, son of Vyas, gained wisdom when still unborn. The communication link between the mother and the unborn baby cannot be denied.

Even when the baby is born, he or she cannot talk or write, but instinctively the baby can communicate the need for milk, warmth and security. Is that not a wonder? We see it every day, but do not look at it as an act of active communication. Soon the mother and the baby adjust to each other's ways and needs, and learn to communicate with each other.

THE GROWING CHILD

As the baby grows and begins to sit, crawl and walk, it also begins to recognise sounds. Ma and Pa are invariably the first sounds it learns to the great pleasure of both the parents. Soon it learns other sounds and associates them with various objects and people around the house. The baby is now a child.

At school the learning process moves on. Using the human instincts, learning is made easier by use of simple colourful objects, pictures, rhythm and music. Little children respond to the rhythm of poems rather than use of plain speech. Music further strengthens use of rhythm and scale. The children respond happily without understanding that simple information is gradually being rubbed into their subconscious mind. This will be the foundation of further learning, and also the development of communication skills later.

The learning process moves on step by step in school. Children learn the languages, use of figures and facts. Many new things are added to the learning curriculum each year. The available information is growing so rapidly that if newer items were not added at the school level, the children would not be able to cope with the needs of the society. This has surely added on to the burden of the children. We hear of learning stress even amongst teenagers. It is like choosing between the devil and the deep blue sea. The need for effective communication at all levels in the society is growing. The new generation will have to adapt itself to handle this burden by learning new skills.

PROFESSIONAL TRAINING

The pressure for learning continues at the college level. There is an explosion of information in every subject at all levels. This explosion needs to be absorbed through training and use of new technologies. Computerisation has made it possible to get a lot of information in a short time. It has also made it possible to communicate all over the world within minutes without having to move out of the home. Better telecommunications and information technology skills have made it possible. It has brought valuable information to our homes and offices.

The laptop and the mobile phone have virtually made it possible to access information anywhere, and at any time. This is the new changing world of communications that was earlier restricted to verbal and written messages. This has been possible in a little over a decade. It is difficult to forecast where we would be in another decade. The only option is to understand how the field of human communication works. We can then improve our skills to become better communicators in everyday life.

COMMUNICATIONS AT THE WORKPLACE

It is a fact that persons who can communicate well do well at the workplace, irrespective of the kind of work they do. At the lower levels where people earn a livelihood through physical labour, the communication skills are not necessary, but at higher levels where the vocation depends upon mental abilities, communication skills are very important.

Teaching

Can you think of a teacher who cannot communicate? If there is one, what is he or she doing in the teaching profession? Teaching requires a very high level of communication ability. Teaching is a profession, which provides livelihood to a very large number of men and women at all levels. This is a worldwide picture. The abilities required at different levels vary greatly. While at the lower levels a teacher performs better not because of personal knowledge, but due to instinctive understanding of little children, who respond to rhythm and to personal attention; an altogether different approach to teach them is required as compared to grown up children. Grown up children and college going youth have different needs of learning. The teachers acquire communication skills accordingly.

Teaching is not limited to school and college going young people only. The explosion in information in every subject has made it necessary for working adults to keep updating their knowledge periodically. This need has made it necessary for the larger companies to have human resource development departments that conduct courses for the personnel. The smaller companies avail the facilities of companies that specialise in adult professional education at the workplace. They conduct seminars to suit the needs of the clients. At every level communication skills are important.

Medicine

Medicine is a highly specialised field where doctors treat sick people. However, the need for communication is not restricted to the patient telling the doctor about his ailment, and the doctor, in turn, prescribing an appropriate treatment. Most patients are unable to communicate the details of their ailment because of their poor skills of communication. The doctors understand this, and ask questions to get the information they require. Besides the one-to-one conversation between the doctor and the patient, additional information is collected through observation and a variety of tests devised as a part of the medical science.

Have you ever visited a nursing home or hospital? You will find that beside the patient's bed there is a complete record of the ailment, the treatment, result of various tests, periodic observations about temperature, pulse, blood pressure, intake of food, bowel movement and the urine passed. The medical record eventually becomes a complete file. Doctors are busy people. Their success depends upon their communication abilities, but with the pressure of work and time, they seek help of support staff, who make the notings in the records. Most doctors write in abbreviated form, many times using their own methods.

It is customary to write once daily, or *bds* to convey that a medicine must be taken twice a day, or *tds* to convey that it should be taken thrice a day. To convey the same to a layman, a doctor may make a bold dot, or two dots separated by a long dash, or three dots with two dashes in between to convey the frequency of the medicines.

Since most doctors fall into the habit of writing abbreviated language and signs, and since laws in developed countries require that hospitals maintain detailed records of treatment, the conversion of the medical jargon into plain language has given rise to a profession of recent origin – medical transcription. This requires knowledge of medical terminology or jargon, and also proficiency in the use of a computer, and has provided employment to many young people around the world.

You can well gauge the importance of effective communication in the medical field not only by appreciating the efforts that go into making the patients' records, but you can visit any department of a hospital, and you will find reports being generated everywhere. Departments of Radiology, Pathology, Cardiology, Orthopaedics, or whatever you have, innumerable reports are generated each day to communicate the status of the patient's condition. Computerisation has helped streamline the preparation of reports, but take communications out, and the field of medicine would come crashing like a house made of cards. Effective communication is the backbone of efficient medical treatment.

Law

Like medicine, the written and the spoken word is the backbone of the legal profession. Have you visited a lawyer's chamber? It is lined from top to bottom with legal books describing case laws. Different aspects of legal problems have been interpreted in a variety of ways, and after much thought, judges have adjudicated upon them, explaining their point of view on the subject. These books provide useful reference material for the lawyers.

Speaking skills draw immediate attention when one hears lawyers argue a case before a judge in the courtroom. Voices go up and down, sometimes in rhythm, and at another time to shock, to highlight salient features of the point of dispute. Words are carefully chosen and used to emphasise a point. Oratorical skills help the lawyer to score. The others just watch as spectators.

Go to a busy court compound in any town. It offers a typically noisy atmosphere with people rushing from one place to another. You will find that literally thousands of documents are written, exchanged or filed each day. People are here to communicate their legal rights in different situations. While the lawyers dictate, stenographers and typists prepare documents. A horde of typists is busy on their typewriters. Computers have invaded this field as much as other fields, but a typewriter that can be carried around is still a tool to ensure a neatly written document. The field of law depends entirely upon communicating through the written and the spoken words. Judges observe body language when an alleged criminal is brought before them.

Engineering and Technology

The field of Engineering and Technology is vast, leading one to factories as well as homes. It touches every aspect of human life – home, workplace and the society. However, once again, the success of this vast field depends entirely upon communication skills, both written and verbal. If it were not for these skills and abilities, human development would have come to a standstill long ago. If mankind is deriving the benefits of better homes, more comfort and leisure, better working conditions and an environment of continuous development, it is due to development in engineering and technology through improved communication abilities.

Selling

Who has not seen a salesperson talking to convince the prospective customer to buy his ware? To reinforce his arguments he presents colourful brochures and testimonials claiming the edge his products have over competitor brands. Whether he succeeds or fails largely depends upon his communication skills. Even when the sale is closed, one continues the communication process by sending reports to the head office and preparing personal records for future use.

The Business Office

Irrespective of the field one pursues through a vocation, the need for good communication skills cannot be overlooked. The typical office is a hub of communication activity. Every day letters are coming and going, inter-office memos are being exchanged, reports are written, presentations are prepared and presented, and a variety of meetings are conducted. Somehow every activity is linked with the ability to communicate.

When one looks at the broader picture encompassing the entire field of professional activities, one begins to appreciate the need to understand both the incoming and outgoing communications. What are the people doing? Most are trying to sell themselves and their products. Others are sharing responsibilities through delegation. Dealing with each other, or rather negotiating each other's points of view is a common. In the same way, some are busy taking decisions. In their own way, each one is using personal communication skills to attain something.

However, very few people really give importance to the subject. Most take it for granted. They feel that it is an inbuilt characteristic in an individual, and that some people are more blessed than others. They do not understand that communication skills can be learnt like any other skill.

> **Think it over...**
>
> The integrity of men is to be measured by their conduct, not by their professions.
>
> — *Junius*

COMMUNICATING AT HOME

Effective communication is equally important at home, as it is in the office. When a couple marries and is physically attracted, the husband and wife think that they possess good communication skills. Gradually, as the physical attraction wears off, the reality comes to the surface.

Effective communication between the husband and wife is very important. When problems surface between a couple, the first thing a counsellor looks for is the breakdown of communication between the two. It has repeatedly been seen that couples that communicate effectively with each other sort out their problems without external interference.

When children grow up, and fail to understand the purpose of the restrictions most parents tend to impose upon them, the situation is described as the generation gap. In reality, the situation signals a breakdown of communication between the parents and the children. This happens because the parents in their earnestness fail to understand the biological and emotional problems the children are going through. On the other hand, the growing children fail to appreciate that the parents know much more about life, and are concerned about the safety and welfare of the children. With each side not being able to appreciate the other's viewpoint, the communication breaks down.

Rather than sitting down and talking it over, both sides go into the silent mode, avoiding discussions lest there should be any unpleasantness in the house.

While breakdown in communication is common in many households, and this explains the frustration of many people, there are many homes where the family members communicate effectively. This promotes harmony and greater understanding amongst the family members. In such homes there is little need to enforce discipline because everyone knows what is accepted, and what is not. Rather than speak, much is conveyed even through a glance or a gesture. This is true even of the people belonging to the same generation. While the young respect the elders, the elders, in turn, appreciate the needs of the younger generation. They guide them through a middle path to find personal fulfilment and happiness. The key to success is good communication.

A TWO-WAY STREET

Effective communication depends upon two individuals, one who is communicating the information, and the other who receives the information. It is important that the person who communicates the information must do it in a way that is understood and acceptable to the other person. However, if the other person is unable to understand the information, or is not willing to accept it, the communication becomes ineffective. For example, if a teacher were to teach a group of children who do not know English, would it help if he taught in English? Of course, it wouldn't. Again, even if the children knew English, and heard what the teacher said, but are unwilling to accept what has been conveyed because they are waiting to go out to play, the children will not benefit from what the teacher has said. It would be a one-way communication. Therefore it will not be effective.

To be effective, a communication must be two-way. It is important that it is presented in a form that is understood by the person receiving the message. Both parties must know the medium of communication. At the same time, the person on the receiving end must be willing to comprehend and accept the message. This is possible only when the circumstances are conducive for both parties to fulfil this responsibility.

This makes it necessary that the person from whom the communication emerges must be aware of the basics of communication skills. It is not enough to say that "my message was very clear," or "I spoke loudly and clearly", or "When Sam understood what I said, why hasn't Bob understood it?" Many factors influence the way people communicate with each other.

When it is necessary that every communication must achieve what is expected of it, one must appreciate that communication skills must be learnt. One must know how people react in different circumstances. It is equally important that one must ensure that the communication is a two-way process. The person on the receiving end must be prepared to react and respond to it. One must also understand that many times people say one thing, and mean quite another. Can that be easily understood? Is that in the interest of good communication?

Think it over...

Little deeds of kindness, little words of love,

Help to make earth happy like the heaven above.

— *Julia A. F. Carney*

ABSENT-MINDEDNESS

When people fail to respond to a verbal message, it is often said that the person is absent-minded. It simply means that the person is inattentive, or even forgetful. One could be inattentive for several reasons. The person may not be interested in what the other person is saying. Even if one is interested, the person may not find the message convincing, and the mind may drift to something else. This happens often at meetings. People are physically present. However, their mind is elsewhere. It is not too rare to see some people sleeping when the speaker is talking through in a meeting. Elderly people lack the power to remain attentive unless the subject is of their special interest. Some also suffer from depression and what is medically known as Attention Deficit Disorder, termed ADD.

One must also understand that when a communication fails at the receiving end, it is not necessarily because the person's attention was elsewhere. This may be because the person deliberately refuses to be influenced by the message. The person may feel that the message is not in his interest, and may deliberately refuse to let it register in the mind. This is common when a person has the habit of sorting out the positive and negative messages he or she receives in everyday life. For example, a teetotaler will not pay any attention to a discussion on making a good alcoholic drink, or a vegetarian to the presentation on a special meat delicacy. During negotiations, when both parties use the best of their communication skills, each knows what is important, and will then refuse to understand or accept the view of the opposite party. This is a deliberate use of blocking a communication. One needs to learn how to get over such obstacles.

COMMUNICATION AND THE INDIVIDUAL

We have seen how one begins communicating from the stage of the unborn baby, and goes on to learn communication skills at school, and then at college. Over a period one learns it through experiences. Some learn the skills well. Most people do not. The lack of communication skills restricts the development and growth of individuals. To make up, many set out to improve their skills. The fact that you have this book before you makes it evident that you are eager to develop your communication skills to get ahead in life.

How is a person affected by lack of good communication skills? Let us begin with the home and family, the basic institution in life. Good communication skills help the person to hold the family together. It means better inter-personal relationships. One can expect a good rapport between the husband and the wife. The children too will respond well when there is harmony between the parents. Relatives and friends also respond well by saying, "we get along well", which can be taken to mean, "we communicate well". Conflicts raise their head only when one begins to overlook the need for freedom of thought and speech. One should accept every person as an individual, and should not thrust one's will on others.

The workplace is a very competitive field for everyone. Everyone is in a hurry to get ahead of the other. Very often many people are equally qualified and skilled. Yet each tries to seek the favour of the boss. In these circumstances, it is the ability to communicate well that makes all the difference.

The position one is able to etch out for oneself in the society depends upon the quality of inter-personal relationship one enjoys with people one comes across in everyday life. Most people overlook the relationships with people like the liftman who serve you, or the guard who stands at the gate, or even the gardener who tends the little garden. People also take the sales assistants at the shops they visit, or even the clerk at the bank they visit occasionally for granted. It is a common experience that good relationships that come from good communication skills improve the quality of life.

What about the one-way communication we convert into two-way by accepting it in the form of the daily newspaper, the magazines we read, and the programmes on the radio, or the news and television serials? We accept them in a big way just as many around us are doing. Mass communication that emerges from a few but is directed to a very large audience extended not only within the country, but also abroad, influences everyone in a big way. Through this media we are also exposed to innumerable advertisements that promise us a better life. How well they do it, is a debatable issue.

This ultimately leads us to one thing. The quality of our life depends upon the quality of communication we respond to. This depends upon our own communication skills, both verbal and non-verbal. This also depends upon our knowledge and understanding of the languages we know. It also depends upon our understanding and interpretation of non-verbal signals, commonly known as body language that gives us an insight into human behaviour.

Let us begin to improve our communication skills by acquainting ourselves with each of these, beginning with the spoken word.

> **Think it over...**
>
> Small kindnesses, small courtesies, small considerations, habitually practiced in our social intercourse, give a great charm to the character than the display of great talents and accomplishments.
>
> — *Kelsey*

POINTS TO PONDER

1. Communication is a vital part of life and living.
2. One must understand the factors affecting communications before becoming a good communicator.
3. Animals communicate just as the plants do.
4. The process of communication in human beings begins before birth.
5. Learning effective communication is an unending effort.
6. Communication plays a vital role at the workplace irrespective of the vocation one pursues.
7. Effective communication is as important at home as it is at the workplace.
8. Effective communication is like a two-way street.
9. The person who receives a message is as important as the person who conveys the message.
10. Effective communication decides the difference between success and failure at home, the workplace and the society.

Using Spoken Words

It is commonplace for humans to understand that communication through spoken words is primarily the principal form of communication. When babies grow up they first uttering words like “ma” and “pa”, which please the mother and the father immensely. At this stage, the baby is not aware of any language, but speaks instinctively. “Ma” and “pa” are common sounds used in the words for a mother and father in many languages.

Children gradually learn the language and dialect that their parents use. They pick up words and sounds that they hear in the household. They repeat sounds as a parrot does. However, soon they begin to construct and use short, simple sentences to converse with the parents and other members of the family. This lesson is carried forward in a play school and later in the kindergarten, when rhyming and rhythm are used to increase the vocabulary. They begin to get the feel of the language.

One does not need to go to school to learn how to use the spoken word. One learns to use it from others who speak. In an environment where everyone is educated and individuals are well mannered and appreciate etiquette, the children learn to speak in a refined form. However, in rustic homes, where the child is exposed to parents and a family that is not educated, the child still learns to use the spoken word, though the form of communication may be somewhat crude and unpolished.

SPOKEN LANGUAGE

All languages emerged initially as spoken languages. A spoken language is the use of words spoken through the mouth by a person to convey something to another person. Through common usage of words by a large number of people, who begin to assign the same meaning to it, a spoken language develops gradually.

The written language follows later, when it becomes necessary to record what has been said. Different means are used to develop the written language. For example, the English alphabet is used not only to write words in English, but is also used in several other languages like French, German and Spanish, using the alphabets to convey the sounds of the spoken language. It is interesting to note that while Hindi and several related languages are written in the *Devanagari varnmala*, or script, Hindi is also written in the Roman script using the English alphabet. This has helped a lot of non-Hindi speaking people to learn the written language easily and in lesser time.

In contrast to the spoken language, the written language follows a system and is refined. Although Hindi is the official language used in many states of India, it is interesting to note that the spoken languages vary in most parts with changed accents and dialects, many times making it difficult for Hindi speaking people to understand what is being said. This is equally true of English that is almost an international language, used freely to develop trade and industry around the world. Even within United

Kingdom, the home of Queen's English, the accents and dialects of the spoken language vary, although the written language is common. The English spoken in U.S.A., Canada, Australia and New Zealand sounds different from the English spoken in U.K.

A language is a living entity. Like human beings, it is undergoing a change all the time. According to the need, human beings 'invent' new sounds and words, or adapt them from other languages according to their requirements. For example, 'guru' is a Hindi word meaning a preceptor, mentor or a spiritual teacher. However, it has now been adapted into written English, meaning an influential teacher or expert, as we see it commonly used as, for example, a management guru. Many such words are being adapted into English and other languages.

Even in Hindi we see a lot of words being commonly spoken in everyday use. For example, 'ticket' is an English word. So is the word 'rail'. Yet we hear of 'rail ticket' being used everyday by millions of people. And what about words like cycle, motor, car, truck and tyre? They are English words, but used extensively in spoken Hindi.

The spoken language is the real language, or the mother tongue, learnt from the parents and the family. It is the authentic language, and has its own grammar and style. The written language is adapted from the spoken language, and is a refined, or a revised version. Even within the same language, the written language has variations in spellings and forms of words, as we see in English used in England and U.S.A. For example, 'centre' is spelt 'center', or 'realise' is spelt 'realize'. This has much to do with the spoken language, and its usage by a large number of people.

> **Think it over...**
>
> All epoch-making revolutionary events have been produced not by the written but by the spoken word.
>
> — *Adolf Hitler*

SPEAKING

To speak means to say something, to communicate some information orally. This is possible with the use of the vocal cords and the vocal apparatus situated in the lower part of the neck in a human being. The study of speech sounds is called phonetics. This is particularly important because one's ability to communicate through the spoken word is greatly influenced by the quality of the sound, the tone and the rhythm, besides the information that is being communicated.

The tone of the voice refers to the musical effect with reference to the pitch, quality and strength of the voice expressing a feeling, emotion or mood. The pitch describes the extent of the sound or tone as high or low. The sound is said to be rhythmic when it follows a strong, regular and repeated musical pattern. This is of special significance when teaching little children to speak. They respond better to rhythmic, musical sounds.

In everyday life, the same words can be interpreted in many ways when the tone of the voice is altered. This fact is widely used in debates and declamation contests. Professionally, legal practitioners are known to use this technique to highlight certain facts, and underplay others, while arguing a case before the judge. In the same way, politicians use their speaking skills to influence the citizens when seeking their support. Public speakers are equally well known to confidently present their point of view before a large audience, to inform, educate or entertain many people through what they have to say.

Religious gurus are known to chant *mantras* and *slokas* to please God, and at the same time reach the message of happiness and bliss to the common man. This is true of all religious preachers, irrespective of the religion they practise or follow. They emotionally move millions of followers through the use of words. Such is the power of speech.

The use and influence of singing, rather than speaking, is known not only to entertain people around the world, but also to arouse them emotionally. We hear devotional singing and music being used in almost every religion around the world. In the same way, singing and music are used to arouse patriotism in the hearts of people, and also motivate armed forces and security services to protect their motherland even at the cost of their lives.

SPEAKING SKILLS

To encourage eloquence in school children, they are taught elocution, the skill of clear and expressive speech. They are encouraged to participate in declamation contests to help develop their confidence and speaking skills. Declamation refers to the act or art of speaking, or reciting, in a dramatic or passionate way. The matter may or may not be written by the child who is speaking. The important thing is to be able to speak clearly, and to control the pitch and the tone of the voice to persuade the listeners to hear and appreciate what is being said. It is common for teachers to select well-written speeches for children to practise speaking skills. Reciting of poems helps add rhythm and emotions to what is said.

Teaching the art of speaking is not new. It dates back to the times of Aristotle and Quintilian. Oratory has always been an important skill for use in private and public life. It was a part of the teaching curriculum in ancient Greece. Earlier, oratory was a great asset to the ministers in the courts of kings and monarchs, but as parliaments developed, politicians found oratory a useful tool to persuade the public and the colleagues alike.

The art of speaking forms a part of learning languages in our schools and colleges. However, it only receives limited attention of the students. Later, as individuals join specific vocations where speaking skills are important, individuals join special classes to develop speaking skills. Many learn the skills through self-study and practise. When a person is able to speak convincingly, he or she is considered intellectually superior. Such is the power of effective communication.

DEBATE

A step ahead of narration is the art of debate, which aims at a formal discussion, where opposing views are presented and argued. The purpose of debate is to consider an appropriate action in a given situation.

Just like declamation contests, children are encouraged to participate in school debates, initially held at class level and later at inter-house level within the school. It is common to have inter-school debates among a group of schools. Later, there would be inter-college debates. This is a useful training for the students at the school and college level, as this takes them a step ahead of plain expression of thoughts to contradiction of opposing thoughts and ideas, and providing an alternate solution.

Since debating is a formal interactive discussion, learning to debate prepares one to speak at clubs and organisations where a variety of opinions are offered. It is also common to have debates in democratic bodies like the local Municipal Corporations, legislative assemblies and parliaments around the world. Noted legislators and statesmen are known to be capable speakers.

Debating in schools and colleges is normally on a given subject where one member of the team speaks in favour of the subject, and the other against it. Since the subject is given in advance and each speaker has a fixed timeframe to speak, the participants prepare the matter in advance. The skills are judged by the way the matter is presented, and also how the speaker deviates from the written speech to challenge what an opposing speaker has said. The lead speakers are allowed additional time to give closing remarks before putting the matter to the house for vote.

When a person is confident about personal debating skills and is knowledgeable, one can participate in extempore debates where the subject is announced just a few minutes before the contest. This gives very little time to prepare, and one relies upon personal knowledge and presentation skills. This is not easy. However, this is the real test of one's knowledge and speaking skills. One develops it by being well informed and through practise whenever an occasion presents itself. This helps develop good communication skills.

Debating opportunities are also provided in schools and colleges through organisation of simulated legislatures such as the Model United Nations, where students represent different countries, or a Mock Parliament, where students represent different political parties and express their opinions on a subject that is relevant on the occasion. Another variation is a moot court and a mock trial for students studying law and similar subjects.

Extempore debating provides a good foundation for young people to participate in group discussions, which form a part of the admission process for many college courses after school. These also provide opportunities to develop the confidence and skills for situations that require negotiations in everyday life. The discussion during study of case histories in a variety of situations also requires the ability to think logically swiftly, and use good speaking skills. Each effort leads to the next, helping to gradually build confidence and skills to face the needs of a successful life.

PUBLIC SPEAKING

Proficiency in declamation and debate lead a person to possess good public speaking skills. Public speaking is a deliberate, structured method to inform, persuade or influence, and sometimes entertain a group of people. Besides communicating information to the audience, public speaking aims at motivating people. The ability to speak well in public is a very valuable skill. History has witnessed the use of this ability for both good and evil. While everyone is aware of gurus and leaders, who are known to have motivated people to good and productive acts in every field, we cannot ignore the evil perpetrated by dictators, many of them very powerful speakers, to have wrecked havoc in the lives of millions of people.

Public speaking dates back to the times when mankind began to use speech as a medium of communication. In ancient Greece, oratory was known to have developed into a fine art. The first known textbook on public speaking is said to be more than 2000 years old. With time, public speaking skills have seen a change towards greater practical usage. Many young people are attracted to develop this ability and seek knowledge by joining institutions that provide training in speaking skills. There are several institutions of national and international repute.

Public speaking is a fine art that many people try to learn but only a few achieve perfection. Capable speakers confirm that they learnt the art through keen observation and by sharpening their skills. A good knowledge of the subject is essential, but ultimately it is the choice of correct words, control over the voice and intelligent presentation, and the correct use of gestures that is important. A good speaker is able to feel the pulse of the audience and uses techniques to draw attention and touch the emotional chord in the mind of the listeners. Using humour to bridge the gap between the speaker and the audience is common, but only capable speakers can do it effectively. Speakers who can hold attention soon develop a relationship with the audience. A very important aspect of public speaking is that a good speaker knows when he has made his point, and stops speaking, leaving the audience thirsting for just 'a little more of it'.

A good public speaker is never just a good speaker. In his or her own right, he or she is a leader. This is natural because speaking skills come only from a high level of knowledge in one or more fields. The knowledge and experience form the foundation. Oratory teaches the presentation skill. Eventually, one is able to communicate well through good public speaking skills.

> **Think it over...**
>
> Three things are required for great oratory: not the orator only, but a great theme and a great occasion.
>
> — *V. Samuel*

MASS COMMUNICATION

A step ahead of public speaking is speaking to audience in a particular region, or to the nation, or even the world. This is known as mass communication, and radio and television are popular media for verbal mass communication. A new addition in this field is the use of telephone, both landlines and mobile phones, for sending messages to people. This way information and messages are conveyed simultaneously to millions of people. Earlier, this was done on a smaller scale by making public announcements on a mobile van, and on a larger scale on the radio. With television reaching the remotest regions, it is now possible to communicate verbal messages, which is further emphasised by visuals for people of all age groups and background. The field of advertising has taken great advantage of this form of communication, and many young people are now opting for various courses to study mass communication.

Recorded music has made it possible for millions of homes around the world to listen and enjoy the music and songs of eminent musicians, from their homes. Recordings are now available in many forms to serve a variety of purposes. This has changed the way people seek entertainment and also spiritual growth through recordings of spiritual hymns, mantras, songs and music.

We have young people learning to serve as radio jockeys or anchors and hosts on television shows. Recording and reproducing a variety of verbal communications is now a specialised field, particularly when the technology in this field has made significant technical advances. To understand and learn more about verbal communication one must carefully hear and analyse the methods used by radio jockeys, anchors and hosts, and also observe visual techniques used to enhance a particular verbal message.

PERSONAL CONVERSATION

By the time a person qualifies from college, he or she is exposed to both speaking and writing skills through variety of ways. The major form of communication is through the spoken word, and is mostly on a one-to-one basis. This may be at home, when one needs to speak to one's parents, the spouse, children or family members. Even at work, most of the talking is on one-to-one basis. However, as one grows vocationally, there is a need for conversing with groups at meetings or during presentations.

A very important issue that needs serious consideration is that although communication begins in human beings before birth and continues after birth, besides the instinctive communication ability, one is taught to speak in many forms and ways, yet most people are unable to communicate effectively. It is not that they do not do it well. They are rather ignorant of the factors that influence verbal communication.

The quality of the voice is an inherited characteristic in human beings. It develops as children pass through adolescence and become adults. While some voices are 'sweet and soothing', there are many others that may be 'shrill and unattractive'. Some voices have rhythm, others sound jarring. Some take to singing naturally, but many fail to sing even after training.

The quality of a verbal message can be greatly enhanced through control over the voice. This is an art that needs to be learnt through great perseverance. Public speakers and singers become effective through a lot of practise.

The choice of the correct words in a message makes it effective. Words that touch the feelings and emotions of the listener register immediately. When the words are dry and cold, they are just like statistics that do not interest a common person. Even when they have been heard, they are ignored as unimportant and extraneous. Good communication skills demand use of appropriate words.

A positive attitude radiates confidence and joy of living. This is something to see and feel, and not hear. When a message comes from a person with such an attitude, a verbal message is effective. Such a person is endowed with a sense of humour. He or she can see a funny side to life. This reflects in the way they speak to others.

Positive people are friendly and accept others as they are, and not as what they would expect them to be. With their friendly temperament such people tend to build a relationship with those they talk to. Their unconscious use of body gestures or signals is open and friendly. This makes the listeners more receptive, and the verbal communication becomes effective.

DIALOGUE

The most common form of verbal communication is referred to as a dialogue. In simple terms, it means a conversation between two or more people. There could be any number of subjects for discussion. The important thing in a dialogue is that at least two persons are involved in sending information to each other. It also means that what one is speaking is being simultaneously understood in whatever form the person perceives the information. The feedback comes in the form of response.

Dialogue is a common form of verbal communication at home, at the workplace and in society in general. Considering its use and importance, one must develop skills to be able to participate effectively in such dialogue.

INEFFECTIVE VERBAL COMMUNICATION

People often wonder why their verbal communication is ineffective even when they make a great effort to ensure that their message is clear. To understand this setback, one must appreciate that the person who conveys a message is not the only person who controls the communication. This person is only one part of the communication. The next part is the content of the message, the information that is being conveyed. The third part is the person to whom the message is conveyed. It could be one person, or even a group of persons. And finally, the test of the effectiveness of the message depends upon the response, or feedback, sent back by the receiver to the person who sent the message.

Every person will emphatically say that he or she sent a message that was 'easy' to understand. It is 'easy' from the point of view of the sender. The words used by the sender may seem easy and commonplace. Even if they were, one cannot be sure that they were correctly pronounced, or that the tone of the voice was conducive for the recipient of the message to understand them correctly.

If every person could correctly put a message into appropriate words, there would be no misunderstanding. There would be no reason for misinterpreting it. Yet, we see it everyday that the courts are full of lawyers who are interpreting words in many ways. The common person also misinterprets words, though on a lesser scale. Every person will agree that he or she has been misunderstood on many an occasion.

The recipient of a message may not have the same interest in the information, as the person who is sending it. The person's mind may be elsewhere when the message is conveyed. Even when a message is heard, it is not necessary that the recipient has also understood it. People interpret the same words to mean differently. If that is so, the message is bound to be ineffective.

Sending a feedback to the sender depends entirely upon the recipient of the message. The person may feel that a feedback is not necessary. The recipient may also feel that since the message was direct, the smile on his face or a nod of the head or acknowledgement of the message is sufficient feedback. It is human nature to presume facts and situations but such presumptions can lead to ineffective communication. Depending upon the nature of the message, ineffective communication can lead to loss of productivity and, in extreme cases, may even lead to failure and loss.

POOR VOICE QUALITY

Poor voice quality is a common cause for poor verbal communication. To a great extent the quality of the voice is an inherited factor but it can be trained for better performance. Cultural differences also influence the way words are pronounced. For example, within India, English pronunciation varies significantly from the north to the south, and from the east to the west. The differences are so marked that it is possible to identify the background of the person who is speaking. Even within the United Kingdom, the home of Queen's English, dialects differ from one area to another, sometimes making it difficult for an average person to understand what is being said.

With people migrating from developing nations to developed nations, they have taken with them their whims and fancies, and also their grammar and pronunciation. With a large number of people using wrong words and phonetics, there is a major difference of opinion amongst language experts whether the changing words must be freely accepted in the language. Those who are in favour of preserving the language in pure form insist that even though speech has been corrupted, the written language must remain pure. Another group insists that the spoken language is the basis of the written language, and the changing words must be incorporated into the language. Only time will tell which way the wind blows.

Speech is greatly influenced by the disorders of the vocal cords, the throat and the lungs. Public speakers and singers take particular care, and do deep breathing exercises to enhance lung capacity and control the voice. Nervous disorders also affect speech. This is common with older people. Some of these problems can be corrected with medical care. One has to live with some conditions. Poor hearing also affects speech quality. With impaired hearing, one is unable to comprehend the correct phonetics, and thereby the speech too is affected. Problems like stammering or lisping are also common, and affect articulation. This could be due to a cleft lip or palate, or to a nervous setback. Partial paralysis too affects the quality of speech. These are childhood problems and can be corrected with timely medical care.

Think it over...

How wonderful is the human voice! It is indeed the organ of the soul. The intellect of man sits enthroned, visibly on his forehead and in his eye, and the heart of man is written on his countenance, but the soul reveals itself in the voice only.

— *Longfellow*

KNOWLEDGE OF THE LANGUAGE

People who travel frequently know how important it is to know the language of the area they visit. The major form of communication when travelling is through the spoken word. However, this is of no avail unless you know the language the person you talk to can understand. Even in India, where as many as 15 languages are recognised, it becomes difficult to converse with people. Hindi and English are common languages, but many times the other person may not understand either of these languages.

In Europe, English is the link language, but many times one is unable to communicate without the knowledge of French and German.

Even with the knowledge of the language, it is necessary to have the ability to choose appropriate words that carry the message effectively. The choice of the words is not easy. Any writer would confirm that. Many people shy away from writing letters because of the fear of choosing wrong words. Choosing words while writing is easier as there is no time limit to put it on paper. While speaking, the choice of words can be difficult, unless one has a good vocabulary of the particular language. In the spoken language the words must flow, because the listener can be impatient if there are gaps in the speech. This can be irritable for the listener, and the verbal communication can fail completely. Every public speaker has faced such situations. One must speak whatever one wants to. To be effective, one must be equipped with appropriate words, and leave the rest to the audience.

EMOTIONAL APPEAL

A quality that stands out remarkably in outstanding public speakers is that they touch the audience emotionally with whatever they speak. Even in everyday dialogue, individuals who can touch the feelings and emotions in others draw immediate attention. The principal reason for this immediate reaction is that the people in the audience feel that the speaker knows how they feel. They can identify their own thoughts in what is being spoken. They see the superiority of the speaker in being able read their thoughts.

Individuals are attracted to songs and music that touches them emotionally, and makes them feel good. It is commonplace to be motivated by patriotic poems and songs. In the same way, devotional songs and music have a relaxing influence, and one is drawn to a higher form of life. Religious leaders all over the world are known to touch the feelings and emotions of the audience when they quote from religious texts and place the audience in a situation where God looks after them.

It is not possible for everyone to touch others emotionally. Only persons who are positive and display confidence can do this. Only virtuous persons who are endowed with great inner strength can move people emotionally. To be effective in this direction it is necessary to develop a magnetic personality. The personal virtues then lend strength to the speech and one is able to touch others emotionally. Of all virtues, love is the greatest and one who can love unconditionally can influence everyone.

Think it over...

One should be free from anger, shun bitter language, should speak only true and sweet words, and avoid talkativeness. One should speak neither more nor less than what is necessary.

— *Swami Dayanand*

POINTS TO PONDER

1. The spoken word is accepted as the primary form of communication.
2. All languages initially emerged as spoken languages.
3. A language is a living entity. It is undergoing change all the time.

4. The spoken word is greatly influenced by the quality of sound, the tone and the rhythm.
5. Speech training begins in the schools through recitation and declamation.
6. Participation in debates helps one to learn the use of logic and selection of correct words to drive home a point.
7. Public speaking is a great art of motivating people in all spheres of life. Many are attracted to it; only a few gain perfection.
8. Mass communication through radio and television has made it possible to reach many people with the least effort.
9. Personal communication is on one-to-one basis, and is used extensively at home; the workplace and the society.
10. Most negotiations are through the spoken word, and two or more people may be involved in the dialogue.
11. Those with poor voice quality should avoid careers where speaking skills are essential to succeed and get ahead.
12. A good knowledge of the language is the basis of good communication between two persons.
13. Emotional appeal makes a message more effective.

Using Written Words

Communicating through the written word follows communication through the spoken word. Millions of people just use the spoken word. They cannot write what they speak. That explains the widespread illiteracy. This restricts growth and development. It also restricts the attainment of the personal potential to grow in one's vocation. The widespread education in every field has led countries to greater development and prosperity. Education based upon the written word, is the key to growth.

Even in everyday life, the use of the written word is important because many of the activities are solely based upon it. A pen and paper are essential tools for every person. The person who can communicate effectively through the written word is immediately recognised for his abilities.

Communicating through the written word has advantages over communicating through speech. While writing, one is under lesser pressure for choice of words. One can think and frame sentences. If you do not like a sentence or a paragraph, you can always re-draft it in another way. You can also experiment with words. You cannot take this liberty when you are speaking to people. Words, once uttered, can never be retrieved. Depending upon the situation, they will be accepted at their face value.

THE WRITTEN AND THE SPOKEN WORD

There is a lot of difference in communicating through the spoken word and the written word. While speaking, the pronunciation and the tone of the voice can significantly influence the meaning. The facial expression, gestures or the body language can also affect the level of effectiveness of the communication. However, when the message is on paper, the possible variations in the meaning are restricted within certain limits. To be precise and specific in conveying a written message, it becomes necessary to have a good working knowledge of the language used by the persons sending and receiving the message.

LANGUAGES

Written communication can be conveyed only through a language. Even when one is unable to speak or hear, one communicates through sign language. The visually handicapped use Braille to read and write. It is estimated that people communicate with each other in as many as 5,000 languages and dialects. Most of these are spoken and rarely written.

King Charles V said, "The more languages a man knew, he was so many more times a man." Each new form of human speech introduces a person into a new world of thought and life.

However, there are a few major languages used by people to transact trade and business around the world. Considering the vast difference between the number of languages used to speak and write, when one gets to communicate through the written word, it is not surprising that there is a fall in the level of effectiveness of the communication.

The secret of effective written communication lies in the knowledge of the language used as a medium of communication. The knowledge of the language, in turn, depends upon how well one knows the grammar and the vocabulary. Developing one's vocabulary may appear to be difficult. But it is not so. It adds to one's strength of expression. Words are to a student, what ammunition is to a soldier. The more you have, the stronger you feel. They are the tools of precise communication. The language of our immediate interest is English.

Think it over...

Language, as well as the faculty of speech, was the immediate gift of God.

— *Noah Webster*

THE ENGLISH LANGUAGE

English is a colourful language. A fair knowledge of this language can get you through almost the whole of the world. It has an estimated 500,000 words, expressing varying shades of meaning. How large is your vocabulary? Some people have a vocabulary of a few thousand words. Most people go through life with a vocabulary of only a few hundred words.

Every individual has two kinds of vocabulary – receptive vocabulary and an active vocabulary. The receptive vocabulary includes words, which you can understand when you hear or read them. The active vocabulary includes words, which you use to express yourself through the spoken and written language. There is always a big gap between the two. Here is your first opportunity to strengthen your vocabulary and improve upon your power of expression. Reduce the gap between your receptive vocabulary and active vocabulary. Utilise more of the words you understand into active use in speech and writing.

Take an interest in words. They make a fascinating study. Make the dictionary your constant companion. Do not hesitate to check up the meaning of any word, which is not very clear to you. Try to learn and use new words everyday. Make a note of them in a small notebook. Review them periodically. Get yourself a thesaurus and a book of synonyms and antonyms. You will be surprised at the range of words that have a similar meaning, and yet the shade of meaning varies for each word. Get yourself a book on increasing your 'word-power'.

Think it over...

To go wrong is natural. To go right is discipline, grammar is the foundation of this discipline in writing.

— *Augustine Birrel*

ENJOY WORDS

Learn to enjoy words. Learn new words. Be clear about their meaning. It will help you differentiate between words that sound similar. This will increase your active vocabulary. You will notice that one word can have several meanings. For example, 'dear' means beloved. It also means costly and expensive. In the same way, 'capital' means wealth. However, the word is also used to specify the city that houses the government of the state or country. The more you study each word, the better you will appreciate the meaning.

To improve your language skills, learn to appreciate the finer meanings of words. It will help you become conscious of finding the right word for the right situation. It will take you a step closer to becoming good at effective communication.

WORDS WITH SIMILAR SOUNDS (HOMOPHONES)

The English language has many words that sound similar, but have different meanings. They can change the meaning of a sentence, a paragraph, or the entire document. Have you ever tried to differentiate between them? The correct use of words immediately shows that the writer knows what he is trying to convey. Here is a list of some words that sound similar or Homophones we come across everyday.

Word	Meaning
Accept	– To receive
Except	– Not including
Adapt	– Make suitable
Adopt	– Choose to take up; take a course of action
Advice	– Counsel
Advise	– To give advice
Affect	– To influence; to have an effect on
Effect	– Accomplish; result; consequence
All ready	– Quite ready
Already	– Previously
All together	– In a group
Altogether	– Wholly
Ante	– Before

Anti – Against
Beside – Close to
Besides – In addition
Canvas – Cloth
Canvass – To solicit
Capital – Wealth, a city; uppercase letter
Capitol – U.S. legislative building
Clothes – Things worn to cover the body
Close – To shut
Coarse – Rough in texture; inferior
Course – A direction taken; onward movement
Compliment – Praise
Complement – That which completes
Council – Assembly
Counsel – Advice; to advise
Consul – A State official in a foreign country
Decent – Moral
Descent – A going down
Dissent – Disagreement
Desert – Barren waste; to abandon
Dessert – A sweet dish eaten at the end of the meal
Diary – A journal
Dairy – An animal farm
Discus – A circular plate
Discuss – To talk
Eminent – Distinguished
Imminent – Impending
Formerly – Previously

Formally – Properly
Fourth – An ordinal
Forth – Forward
Hear – To perceive
Here – In this place
Instance – An example
Instants – Moments
Lesson – An exercise
Lessen – To diminish
Lose – To suffer loss
Loose – Not firmly fixed in place
Passed – Past tense of 'pass'
Past – A former time
Personal – Private
Personnel – Persons
Proceed – Go on; make one's way
Precede – To go before
Presents – Gifts
Presence – Being present
Principal – Chief
Principle – Fundamental source; basic rule
Quiet – Still
Quite – Completely
Respectfully – With respect
Respectively – In order
Right – Correct
Write – To record
Rite – A ceremony

Sight	– A view
Site	– A location
Cite	– To quote in support of a position
Stationery	– Paper; writing material
Stationary	– Not moving
Than	– Conjunction used in comparison
Then	– At that time
Their	– Belonging to people
There	– In that place
They're	– Contraction of 'they are'
Threw	– Past tense of throw
Through	– By way of
Thorough	– Exact
To	– Preposition (indicates movement towards a person, place or thing)
Too	– Adverb (in addition)
Two	– A number
Weak	– Not strong
Week	– Seven days
Weather	– Climate
Whether	– Conjunction (introducing indirect question expressing doubt or choice between alternatives)

SPELLINGS

Another aspect closely linked to the subject of similar sounding words is that of use of correct spellings. You have noticed how meanings differ with change of an alphabet in a word. For example, effect and affect. Both words have altogether different meanings. Even when words are not similar sounding, correct spelling of words is very important. One learns words through usage. Correct spellings too are learnt with usage. Whenever in doubt, use a dictionary.

PUNCTUATION

Most people give little attention to punctuation marks. They feel it is not important. Punctuation marks are considered a mystery that can be overlooked and forgotten. As long as a sentence ends with a full stop, is it important what other punctuation marks really mean?

Punctuation marks help make the meaning of written words clear. Most people are aware of punctuation marks, but do not know how to use them. There are as many as 30 marks, but only a few are in common use. Too much punctuation is as bad as no punctuation. The best rule in using punctuation is to use common sense.

Correctly used, punctuation marks add vigour and clarity to the written work. They help to separate words and ideas, group and keep together related ideas, and set aside words that need special emphasis. They are not difficult to use provided you understand their use. Their use is not intended to give a broken look to a communication. It is to improve the clarity and effectiveness of the message. Here is some quick revision on use of punctuation marks.

The full stop (or Period) (.): The full stop is used

1. At the end of a sentence.
   For example, *Thank you for coming to meet me.*
2. After an abbreviated word.
   For example, *Mr. Mrs. Dr. V.P.P. C.O.D.*

However, it is not used

- when abbreviations represent certain organisations such as *WHO, ICAR, UNICEF, IARI,* etc.
- when the abbreviation is for a currency as *Rs, $* or *Yen.*
- when a name is abbreviated as Sam for Samuel, or *Anu* for Anuradha.
- when abbreviations such as *memo, exam* or *math* are used instead of full words.

3. After a number or letter in an outline, such as

   A.

   1.

   2.
4. After a fragment or incomplete sentence, such as

   Hello, good morning.
5. In groups of three when words are eliminated, as

   "...is sturdy, easy to use and long-lasting."

The comma (,): The comma is perhaps the most misused punctuation mark. It denotes a short pause in reading, and divides a sentence into parts according to construction. For example, *The final year students, stepping forward as a group, conveyed gratitude to the teachers with a bow and a loud "thank you".*

It is also used to separate individual nouns and adjectives. For example:

1. The cameras, films, albums and photo paper were dispatched through courier.
2. May God bless the couple with a long, happy and prosperous wedded life.

The comma is also used in many other ways. For example, when writing the date – June 27, 2007 or after a salutation in an informal letter and the complimentary close in all cases – My dear Rita, Yours sincerely or Yours very truly.

Use a comma whenever you feel it will make the meaning more clear. Do understand its proper use. Do not sprinkle it as though it were an ornament in a communication. A good rule is that whenever in doubt do not use it.

The semi-colon (;): A semi-colon indicates a greater break in thought than a comma, but lesser than a full stop. It is best used when the second half of the sentence depends upon the first half, and the two parts are connected with the word *for.* In such cases *for* can be eliminated, and a semi-colon used. For example, *We cannot accept you for this position; a Master's degree is an essential qualification.*

The colon (:): The colon indicates a little longer pause than the semi-colon. It divides the sentence into two or more parts, each complete in itself. It also precedes a quotation. For example,

1. *Your salesman clearly said: "Please accept the offer as it is, or leave it."*
2. *I am not surprised that you let me down: I was expecting it.*
3. *Dear Mr. Baker:* or *Dear Sir:*
4. *We ordered for the following: 2 cases of detergent powder, 3 cases of toilet soap and 1 case of scouring powder..*

The exclamation mark (!): This mark is used to express strong emotion, satire, doubt, surprise or irony.

Some tend to use it excessively. If you can remember that it is an 'exclamation' mark, you will know when to use it. A good rule: use it sparingly. Do not use a comma in the sentence when you use the exclamation mark. For example, *The information sent by you is shocking. We can hardly believe it!*

The question mark (?): The question mark is used at the end of a sentence, which asks a question. For example, *Could you please suggest how I can be more effective?* It can also be used within brackets to express doubt or uncertainty. For example, *We expect to complete the work by November 30 (?) if peaceful conditions continue.*

The hyphen (-): The hyphen is used to join two parts of compound words. For example, *warm-hearted; three-fifth.* It is also used with prefixes such as ex, self, all and the suffix elect. For example, *Ex-captain; self-confidence; All-India; secretary-elect.*

The dash (–): The dash is used to indicate a dramatic pause. For example, *We had your order ready – in just two days!* It is also used to indicate omission of certain words or letters. For example, *Mr. – was present in the office that day. He called him a r – l.*

Parentheses ( ): Parentheses are used when words, which are not a part of the sentence, are inserted into it to give an informal and confidential effect. For example, *Your salesman (is he aggressive?) was very confident about the quality of your products.*

Parentheses are also used to enclose numbers, references, directions and question marks. For example, *You may please (1) check the balance payable by you, (2) obtain a draft for the sum on Punjab National Bank, and (3) dispatch it to us through a reliable courier. You can clear your doubts by referring to our standard terms of business printed on the reverse side of the order form (please see items 6, 7 and 8).*

Quotation marks (" "): When certain words that are not those of the writer need to be included, they are enclosed within quotation marks. For example, *Your salesman had emphatically said, "The order will definitely be executed within a week."*

In certain cases, when words are enclosed within quotation marks, they can by expression of doubt change the meaning of the word, and cause offence. For example, *We are amused that you talked of 'integrity' and 'honesty'.*

Single quotation marks are also used to enclose a quotation within a quotation.

Apostrophe ('): The apostrophe is used to indicate the possessive case, and to denote the ommission of a word. For example, *It is Sushil's duty to look after the office record. It's time to go* is written instead of *It is time to go.* In the same way, *isn't* is used for *is not*, or *won't* for *would not.*

Ditto marks ("): Ditto marks imply repetition.

For example, 20 pieces of toilet soap.
20 " " detergent cake.
10 " " scouring cake.

WRITING LEGIBLY AND NEATLY

One of the first few language skills taught to a child is to write legibly and neatly. The children are compelled to do so initially. With time, when nobody checks them, many begin to scribble. Unfortunately, many young people feel that it is the privilege of the adults to scribble. Nothing could be farther from the truth.

A good neat handwriting is a great asset if you want to communicate effectively. Even when you word your message carefully, if your handwriting is not legible and cannot be read easily, can you blame the person it is directed to for not being able to understand it? This is a common problem with many people. Their handwriting lets them down.

A good presentation is equally important. If the handwriting is legible, but the presentation is not neat, the reader's attention may be distracted. He is likely to misunderstand or misinterpret the message. To improve handwriting and neatness skills, one must be conscious of the need and practise it in everyday life. Try to write neatly all the time. You will not need to strain yourself when you are writing an important letter or document.

SOME SIMPLE RULES

When writing, use these simple rules:

- Use a language that the target reader can easily understand. Academicians may appreciate high-flown language, not the common person.
- Do not use abbreviations, or words or phrases used by specific professionals and experts. The common reader may not understand them.
- Use words that are easily understood. While choosing between two words, select one that is easier to understand. For example, book, tome, volume and publication have similar meanings, but 'book' is the easiest to understand.
- Write to the point. While writing, one tends to deviate from the subject.

- Let the matter progress logically, just as B follows A, and C follows B.
- Write in as few words as possible. After you have written, revise the text to condense it by keeping the essentials, and trimming the frills.
- Do not write what the reader already knows.
- Avoid clichés.
- Avoid unnecessary phrases. Use simple words. For example, 'in the event of' could be replaced with 'if'.
- Write with a positive outlook. Always avoid the negative.
- If you have written what you wanted to, just stop. Revise.

ORGANISE YOUR WRITING

To get organized for writing, follow these simple steps:

- Get a supply of blank cards – 3 inches by 5 inches.
- Write one idea, or lead-point, on each card.
- Put together the cards into lots – one lot for one group of thoughts.
- In each lot, sort out the cards according to priority, the most important card on the top. The ideas must be in logical order.
- You now have the ideas ready to be developed. This system allows direction as well as flexibility of writing.

WRITING SKILLS

Most people hesitate to write. They fear that they may not be able to write well. People restrict their own development with imaginary fear. The truth is that everyone can write well, provided one is willing to learn the simple techniques of writing. You are no exception. Believe in your personal abilities. Self-confidence will help you grow.

The moment most people sit down to write they become so self-conscious that they just blank out. Gradually one recollects thoughts, but the thinking may remain stilted for a long time until the tension fully wanes away. Relax! Take a rough paper. Imagine that the person you wish to communicate with is sitting across the table. Unfortunately, he cannot hear. You need to convey your message to him in writing. Write as you would speak.

What is the message? Note down each point that you would like to make – just as though he was sitting before you and you were talking to him. Have you got all the points right? Now mark them in order of preference by placing 1, 2, 3 and so on against each. When you finally present the points to the individual, you would want to have the most important one on the top. Once you have the priorities sorted out, you can prepare the final written note.

While speaking, one can attract the attention of the other person in several ways. However, when you convey a message by writing it, there is only one way to attract attention. Make the introduction attractive. It must arouse the interest of the other person. He should feel like reading further. He must get to know the topic at the outset.

Divide the ideas or points into paragraphs. Proceed logically. Put one point in one paragraph. Common points can be put together in a paragraph. Write short paragraphs. They make the matter more readable. Use simple words. Write short sentences. The paragraphs should be crisp and easy to understand. As you write, ask yourself: Is my message clear? Is it concise? Is it convincing? Is it complete? When you answer 'yes' to these questions, you have done your best.

Your 'best' need not necessarily be the last word on the subject. Let us not forget: there is always a better way of doing the same thing. If it were not so, all progress would come to a stand still. Therefore, make it a habit to revise what you have written. Again ask yourself: can I improve upon it? If you can, go ahead and do it. Let your work bear the stamp of perfection.

All this sounds simple. But writing in itself is a technique. One learns it only through practice. It involves knowledge of the language, good communication skills, and the ability to think in terms of how others will interpret the words and expressions used. The more you write, the sooner you will learn the techniques that work. Observe the work of others. Look for the best. Adapt ideas to suit your style. Soon you will have a writing style of your own.

Think it over...

The writer does the most who gives his reader the most knowledge, and takes from him the least time.

— *Sydney Smith*

COMMUNICATING THROUGH LETTERS

Millions of letters of all descriptions are written each day by an equally large number of people all over the world. People living in the remotest of places need to write and receive letters. The letters may communicate ideas and thoughts between relatives, friends, business associates and others. Many letters cross the barriers of countries, carrying vital messages, seeking a reasonable response.

Most people, including the educated lot shirk from writing letters. Many do it only to fulfill their responsibilities at the workplace or the society. Only a small minority does it for the great pleasure they derive out of it. However, we cannot ignore that letters play a significant role in the lives of most people. If one must get ahead, the ability to write effective letters will promote greater efficiency and happiness in life.

It is the small fraction of people who promote trade and business, and cordial and friendly relationships between people. If there could be more effective letters, trade and business would grow around the world. People would attain greater success and happiness.

Most people feel that writing a good letter is a natural gift. Only a few are so blessed and can write good letters. It is true that a few learn the art quickly, many times without even a conscious effort. In reality, everyone can learn to write an effective letter – one that serves the purpose for which it is written.

Writing a letter is not like writing a story or an article for a publication. Both have a different purpose. A letter is a communication from one person to another whereas a story or an article is a message from one person to many unknown people. Even though both have some similarities, each needs a different kind of treatment. The art can surely be learnt through some effort.

Think it over...

I have made this letter longer than usual, because I lack the time to make it shorter.

— *Blaise Pascal*

WRITING A GOOD LETTER

A good letter can get many things done for a person. It can get one a call for a job interview, help sort out a problem or even create better relations. If you feel incapable of writing one, it is never too late to learn how to write a good letter.

Most letters are mundane. Some are even stupid, because no thought has gone into writing them. A few are first rate. They are a treat to read, and re-read.

A good letter is simple and yet it conveys a message in a few common everyday words. It sounds natural. It is specific. It is neither dull, nor pedantic. It uses more of nouns and verbs than adjectives. It exudes a positive attitude towards the subject.

The secret of good writing is to be specific and brief. After the letter has been written, it must be revised. The frills must be trimmed off through ruthless editing. The last paragraph must tell the reader what you want. Specify what the reader needs to do or what you intend to do. After you have conveyed your message just stop.

A good letter must be neatly written or typed on a business-size paper. The matter should preferably be restricted to one page and broken into paragraphs to make reading easier. The important words may be underlined, highlighted or typed in bold font.

Enclose the letter in an envelope that has the recipient's address neatly typed, or hand written, on the right lower end of the envelope. Do not forget to mention the postal code for easy delivery. The sender's identity must be written on the left upper or lower end of the envelope.

WRITING AN EFFECTIVE COMMUNICATION

For effective written communication, one must remember the five Cs. The communication must be:

1. **Clear:** It must tell clearly what is to be done.
2. **Concise:** If it is lengthy, the real purpose of the message may be lost in the words.
3. **Courteous:** It has been observed that requests promote action sooner than an order.
4. **Convincing:** Unless the reader is convinced that the request needs to be acted upon, the communication will remain ineffective.
5. **Complete:** If the communication leaves behind an element of doubt, it will not be complete. Action will not be forthcoming.

There is another school of thought, which suggests that to make a communication effective, one must remember the ABC of writing.

A is for attention. The communication must immediately attract the attention of the reader. Unless the person is attentive, no action can be expected.

B is for brevity. The message should be as brief as possible. It is easy to get lost amongst words if the message is lengthy.

C is for convincing. Unless the person is convinced of the need for action, the message will fail to be effective.

There is yet another straightforward way of promoting effectiveness in a written message. The message must specify not only who should perform the desired action, but also:

What is to be done?

How it is to be done?

When it is to be done?

Where it is to be done?

Why it is to be done?

When the communication answers all of the questions, nothing is left to doubt. The effective communication gets results.

> **Think it over...**
>
> Reading maketh a full man; conference a ready man; and writing an exact man.
>
> — *Francis Bacon*

A STYLE IN WRITING

No two writers will write the same thing in a similar way. Both the messages may convey the same thing, but each is likely to sound different. This is because each person has a particular style of writing. It is this style, which differentiates one writer from the other. The writing style does not develop overnight. It comes gradually as one writes, and re-writes the same thing. It reflects the way a person wants to put across the thoughts. Since each person thinks differently, the style of writing too is bound to be different.

Pick up two different newspapers. The two will obviously carry similar news. However, you will observe that one newspaper is different from the other. In the same way, two television channels may be relaying the same news, but they are different. The reason is obvious. Each newspaper and news channel has its own style, and maintains it from day to day.

People who receive a lot of mail or deal with several companies, will confirm that the communication from each company has a style of its own. In business correspondence, the corporate writing style gets preference over individual writing style until it serves a special purpose. Individuals use the personal style within the sanctions of the corporate style.

How can one define 'style' in writing? Perhaps it is easier to feel and understand it rather than define it in words. While writing, the words not only convey the meaning of the message, but they also create a rhythmic effect, which can be pleasing or sometimes not so. The written words reflect the thoughts and the attitude of the writer.

A novice tends to become conscious the moment he or she sits down with a paper and pen to write. The mind turns blank and cannot convey the intended message. Even when the person comes out of the initial state of shock of having to put one's thoughts on paper, the person produces 'cold' words on paper, and not a personal message!

While learning to write and develop a personal style, a person must understand that a style is very personal and to develop it, one must truly be the personal self and not somebody else. To be able to do so, one must resolve to be natural and comfortable with what one is, and not copy someone else.

Most people are guilty of copying others. If one were to observe people and adapt ideas how they succeed and live better, it would be appreciated. However, when one copies style blindly, as in clothes, mannerisms and writing, it does not take long to see and feel the lack of originality. To be original and convincing, the simple secret is: "be yourself!"

Write, as you would speak – in plain simple words, directed at the person you are talking to. If you can speak convincingly, you should be able to write equally convincingly. It is not as simple as it sounds, because good writing requires imagination and technique. However, do not let that frighten you.

Observe how the newsreader gives out the news on radio and television. The message is brief, crisp and clear, without any frills.

Pick up the newspaper and note how messages are conveyed in as few words as possible. Much information is communicated in just a few lines. Observe the simplicity of the words and the sentences. To emphasize the message, the newspaper may carry a photograph, or even a graphic illustration.

There is no magic formula to develop a personal style of writing. It will develop over a period of time, as you make a conscious effort to write in conformity with the writing techniques already discussed.

GRAPHIC SKILLS

Few people possess good graphic skills. These skills may not be necessary in everyday life. However, the ability to communicate graphically can greatly enhance the value of written communications. Each day graphic skills are becoming more important. Illustrations help impart information quickly. Many newspapers and magazines are doing it everyday. It is said a good picture is worth a thousand words. An illustration adds to the effectiveness of written reports. It drives home the point immediately. With the advancement of information technology and availability of laptop computers and LCD projectors, it is becoming commonplace to make visual presentations with verbal explanations. This makes it necessary to develop skills in this field. The only way to learn graphic skills is through practice. Use illustrations wherever you feel they improve the effectiveness of the communication.

POINTS TO PONDER

1. Communicating through the written word follows communication through the spoken word.
2. Written communication can be conveyed only through a language.
3. A fair knowledge of the English language can get a person through almost the whole of the world.
4. Language skills depend upon the knowledge of words.
5. Similar sounding words can be confusing to use.
6. Words can be misinterpreted if the spellings are wrong.
7. Punctuation marks help make the meaning of the written words clear.
8. A communication must be written legibly and neatly.
9. To be effective, follow the simple rules of writing.
10. To write sensibly, the writer must be well organized.
11. Writing skills develop gradually through practice.
12. Letters play an important role in the lives of all people.
13. Writing a letter can be simple if you learn the basics.
14. To make a written communication effective, remember the 5 Cs.
15. Everyone has a personal style of writing.
16. Illustrations always enhance the value of written communication.

Body Language

Most people are mistakenly under the impression that communication refers to the spoken or the written word; that it is restricted only to the various languages spoken and written around the world. This is not true. Besides speaking and writing, everyone is communicating through the body, even without being conscious of it. This is referred to as body language. As an individual interested in effective communication, one must understand it better.

It is not that people are totally unaware of body language. Who has not seen a young girl blush at the mention of marriage? Who has not seen a person turn pale and have trembling legs when asked to speak in public without prior notice? Who has not seen a person break down on receiving tragic news? Everyone has seen these and many more examples of how the body reacts in a particular situation. However, most people are not aware how information can be utilised to make communication more effective. This knowledge is useful in developing self-confidence. It can also be a guide in handling individuals during discussions and negotiating deals.

SIGN LANGUAGE AND BODY LANGUAGE

Sign language and body language is not the same

thing. A sign language uses manual communication instead of sound and words to convey a message, using hands, arms or the body and facial expressions to convey the thoughts. Deaf people use sign languages, many of which are similar. Despite minor differences, deaf people can effectively communicate through them. Body language refers to the natural response of individuals to situations. Some refer to it as involuntary body language. Voluntary body language would mean intentional movement, expressions and gestures to deliberately convey a message.

Communicating through signs is not restricted to the deaf or those incapable of speaking. We see it in many forms in everyday life. In cricket, the umpire indicates a 'four' by waving his hand horizontally; a 'six' by raising both his hands. He declares a batsman out by raising his finger. In other games like football and hockey also the umpires use signs. When driving, the driver uses signs to indicate movement to the left or right, or that he is slowing down, or coming to a stop. Strangely, people raise their hands up as sign of surrender. Students raise a hand in class to seek permission to speak.

In everyday life, Hindus greet by joining the palms of the hands. Some offer respect by touching the feet. The other person reciprocates with blessings by placing the hand on the head or shoulder. American Indians are known to greet by raising the hand to show an open palm accompanied by the sound: "How!" Many greet by waving the hand. Some greet with an embrace or a hug or a kiss on the cheek or forehead. In some areas people greet by rubbing the noses. All these are intended to mean: I am pleased to see you.

> **Think it over...**
>
> Learning non-verbal communication is to learn to give meaning to gestures we observe in everyday life.
>
> — *Anon*

OBSERVING BODY LANGUAGE

Earlier, we discussed that though unaware about it, people are communicating all the time. It is for individuals to understand and give a meaning to these communications. Although these communications are non-verbal, they project both positive and negative feelings. The positive feelings are visible as enthusiasm, joy and happiness. The negative feelings manifest as boredom, loneliness and also as anger and frustration.

To observe how people communicate through their body, observe the way people behave at a railway station, or a bus terminal. You can also carry out the exercise at the airport. Only the class of people will be different. You will see people rushing about – some are anxious, others may be lonely or bored. Those on a vacation, or important assignments will be enthusiastic and happy. Sitting peacefully, observe how people dress, walk about or sit reading a magazine. Observe how they talk or look at each other. From their body postures try to guess what one could be saying to the other.

In the same way, observe children in a school. Observe how they talk to each other. Observe how they greet teachers or parents visiting the school. Observe their reactions to different situations. Try to figure out how they feel. Why do they behave as they do? You will gradually begin to understand body language.

Have you observed people in a hospital waiting room, or those sitting outside the Intensive Care Unit? Can you read the anxiety and the fear on their face? Have you observed the joy and happiness on the face of the people leaving the same hospital with a newborn baby child? You can observe all kinds of emotions being communicated to you unconsciously. When you begin to understand them, you begin to understand how to react or deal with them. Your communication in response becomes more effective.

ANALYSE THE SIGNALS

Next to observation is analysis. You must be able to analyse what you have observed. You cannot come to any conclusion on the basis of one body movement or reaction. Each movement is referred to as a gesture. It is to be observed that a gesture does not come alone. Gestures come in groups. These gestures are linked with personal attitudes. For example, if a person is nervous, the face may turn pale, the hands may tremble and there may be sweat on the brow. In the same way, if a person is exposed to a ghastly scene, the person may close the eyes tightly and cover the mouth with the hand to stifle a shriek.

When you observe a person's gestures, observe your own gestures as well. Without knowing it, your gestures may be influencing the other person. This is observed in a husband–wife relationship, and also between a parent and a child.

When you identify a group of gestures, give a meaning to each gesture, and then analyse the group as a whole. Accurate evaluation cannot be learnt overnight. One needs to persevere through hits and misses. With effort, the observation becomes keen. With some thought, the evaluation too becomes accurate. A person needs to observe self-restraint after analysing the gestures. A hasty reaction may not be right. It is better to think, consider motives and possible reactions, and then react. This way the feedback is always effective.

VOLUNTARY AND INVOLUNTARY GESTURES

While observing body gestures and later analysing them, it is necessary that a person must be able to differentiate between voluntary and involuntary gestures. In learning body language one looks for physical reactions to situations. In the normal course, these reactions are involuntary. They happen without the person being aware of them. Taking a cue from them, the other person responds.

However, all gestures may not be involuntary. Who has not seen a child pretending to have a stomachache to avoid eating something he does not like? His gestures compel the mother to think twice before forcing him to eat. In the same way, who has not seen an employee pretending to be sick, so that he can go on leave to attend a wedding in the family? Even in everyday life, appreciating the effect of body language, people make voluntary gestures to mislead others. This is very important when negotiating business. One should not react immediately to the gestures. In observing body language, it is necessary to evaluate whether the cluster of gestures in voluntary or involuntary.

THE FACIAL EXPRESSION

The face identifies a person first and foremost. It is often said: the face is the index of the mind. With the mind controlling the whole body, one can appreciate the importance of the expression on the face. Without a word, on meeting a person, it is not uncommon to hear people say:

- "He looked as though he could eat you."
- "He looked invitingly."
- "I could see he needed me."
- "He did not want anyone to come his way."

The facial expression is a combination of the reactions of the eyebrows, the eyes, the nose, the lips and the chin. The skin also plays a role when it flushes, or turns livid, or folds to frown. It also sweats. Dimples too are expressive. The face expresses all kinds of emotions ranging from love to fear. Equally so, it expresses anger, greed and hatred. Facial expressions change just as the situations change. This can be easily observed when you call a child honest and hardworking or demoralise him by calling him a cheat or a thief. The adults too react to these statements quickly. The face is self-expressive.

By observing the facial expression, one can appreciate how the other person feels. This gives a salesman an opportunity to close a sale. It gives the businessman an opportunity to negotiate a deal or the public speaker to understand how the public is reacting to what he is saying. When things are not going right, it gives a person an opportunity to change his strategy and still emerge a 'winner' in the end.

> **Think it over...**
>
> Looks are more expressive and reliable than words; they have a language, which all understand, and language itself is to be interpreted by the look, as well as tone with which it is uttered.
>
> — *Tryon Edwards*

THE SMILE

To smile means to form one's features into a pleased, friendly or amused expression, with the corners of the mouth turned up. It is also said that a smile is the easiest way to improve one's looks. A smile is associated with joy. With an eye contact, a smile communicates a greeting to a friend or an acquaintance. A big, broad smile communicates victory and happiness. But we also hear, "He was smiling by himself", meaning he was amused. Not all smiles indicate joy. A smile could also indicate conceit and defiance. Sometimes, a smile expresses sarcasm. Watch out for the smile on the face of the person you are talking to.

SMOKING

Smoking is closely related to the lips. Despite health warnings, many people smoke cigarettes, cigars, *biris* and the pipe. It has been observed that people smoke when they need to think. To seek co-operation, smokers offer a cigarette to the other person. This serves a dual purpose. It serves an opportunity to 'share something' with the other party, and also serves as a 'thinking crutch'. This is also an expression of friendship and courtesy.

Many people keep looking at the cigarette as though they are trying to read something on it. They are really in deep thought. Others close their eyes as they puff, using a cigarette as a tranquilliser to soothe the nerves. When relaxed and happy, they may make smoke rings.

When smokers need to concentrate, they draw longer at the cigarette or *biri,* retain the smoke longer and exhale it slowly only to take another puff. After the initial thinking, the smoker makes decisions quickly to get over whatever was being discussed. However, pipe smokers take longer, playing 'hide and seek' to give a personal identity to the conversation.

EYE CONTACT

Eyes are more expressive than the lips. The size of the pupils changes with the emotional state of a person. Strong emotions and moods stimulate the sympathetic nervous system and cause the pupils to dilate. A state of fear also affects the appearance of the eyes.

Eye contact refers to two persons looking into each other's eyes at the same time. If an interest is aroused, then the pupils tend to dilate, making the eye contact intense. Mothers are often seen to communicate with their children through eye contact. In a well-knit family, it is not unusual for the members to communicate through eye contact, which is symbolic of personal involvement and intimacy.

In the normal course of a conversation, people look at each other for 30 to 60 percent of the time. When it is beyond 60 percent, one may be more interested in the person rather than the conversation. One makes a longer eye contact when listening, rather when talking. Eye contact is said to improve retention of what one hears, and therefore facilitates the process of learning.

Eye contact varies amongst people of different cultures. For example, in many cultures, people look down when speaking to an elder or superior person. In some cultures, women do not look directly into the eyes of the in-laws and relatives who are older. In some regions, continued eye contact with elders and seniors is looked upon as an aggressive act. In other regions lack of eye contact may be considered as being less trustworthy. People who make eye contact easily are accepted as 'more open'.

One often hears of a person 'stealing a look'. It refers to a sidelong glance at a person without being caught at it. We also hear of a person 'giving someone the eye', meaning the person has expressed interest through eye contact. It is equally common to hear the threat, "he dare not look this way", or "I have seen many like him." Celebrities are often seen wearing dark glasses to hide their eyes.

Young people flirt with the eyes. A look into the eyes expresses mutual interest. Young people may look from the edge of the eyes at each other, or may have their eyes locked as they look at each other in a crowd.

When observing people, look into their eyes. You will learn much from their expression. Think about it. Analyse the reactions. Soon you will be analyzing the communication to your advantage.

> **Think it over...**
>
> A beautiful eye makes silence eloquent: a kind eye makes contradiction an assent; and an enraged eye makes beauty deformed. – This little member gives life to every other part about us.
>
> — *Joseph Addison*

USING SPECTACLES

Many people wear spectacles that somewhat hide the eyes, but not completely so. The spectacles or the reading glasses communicate messages that may lead one to understand the person and the situation better. Who has not seen people playing with their glasses? They take them off, place them on the table, wipe the lenses, and again put them on. These gestures suggest that the person is seeking time to think, to consider whatever you might have said.

When a person looks over the spectacles dropped on to the lower bridge of the nose, and has the eyes slightly closed, it means that the person is trying to concentrate upon the person to scrutinise the situation. It also means that he is trying to seek a solution to the problem. Many senior executives and lawyers are known to use these gestures, particularly when they are with the subordinates or deeply studying a problem.

When a person takes off the glasses and points them towards the door, he is showing the way out. It is also not unusual to see a person removing the glasses and throwing them on the table. This is a threatening gesture.

You will see judges and lawyers using it in a courtroom. The gesture intends to express: "you are going beyond limits". It may also be an expression of resistance. It is a sure signal that one needs to change one's strategy. The approach to the subject must be changed. You could perhaps present your viewpoint in another way.

THE EYEBROWS

The strip of hair growing on the ridge above a person's eye socket is called the eyebrows. The eyebrows are as expressive of human emotions as are the other parts of the face. Who has not heard, "He raised his eyebrows when I told him about it?" Raised eyebrows express surprise and mild disapproval. They can also mean envy and disbelief.

THE NOSE

The nose is yet another expressive part of the face. It is associated with breathing and is directly connected with life. A person dies when the breathing stops. The nose is also associated with the sense of smell. It reacts immediately to good and bad odours. Whereas fragrances turn a person 'on', it is not surprising to see people turn 'off' when the atmosphere smells foul.

Go to a big party and observe people serve and eat food. The expression on the nose will tell you what item on the menu is good, and which is not. Turning up the nose universally describes dislike and rejection. Babies also turn up their nose when they disapprove of food placed before them.

The nose also expresses emotions like anger. Just as an angry bull snorts, an angry person takes shorter breaths with the nostrils enlarged. The breathing resembles snorting. When this is accompanied with scratching the back of the head, it can reflect the feeling of frustration. Taking deep breaths, exhaling slowly with a sighing sound also reflects disgust and frustration. The flushed colour of the nose skin expresses a state of embarrassment.

When a person finds it difficult to take a decision, he may pinch the nose at the bridge with the eyes closed. This means that he is about to come to a conclusion. When a person touches or rubs the nose, it means that the person is in doubt. He may not agree to the proposal. When negotiating a proposal, this can be a valuable signal in that one can make a new offer, or even amend the existing proposal.

THE CHIN

The chin, the part of the face below the mouth, also communicates messages. Who has not been advised, “Keep your chin up” meaning ‘remain cheerful’, even if the going is tough. Some would suggest, “take it on the chin” meaning ‘accept the problems without complaining’. Tightening of the jaw muscles and pushing the chin out indicates defiance. Rubbing the chin during a conversation means that the person is trying to evaluate the facts. Stroking a beard also has a similar meaning.

> **Think it over...**
>
> A beautiful smile is to the female countenance what the sunbeam is to the landscape; it embellishes an inferior face, and redeems an ugly one.
>
> — *Johann Kaspar Lavater*

THE HEAD

Just as the facial expressions communicate feelings and emotions, the position of the head is also expressive. For example, when a person tilts the head forward, he means that he is trying to be attentive. He wants to listen better. This can be an important indication to the speaker that the audience is attentive. When excessive information is conveyed and the audience cannot assimilate it, the audience becomes disinterested. When the head is held casually, it indicates lack of interest.

THE HANDS

The most popular form of using the hands is to convey greetings. In India, raising the arms people join the palms of the hand to say, "*Namaste*" or "*Namaskar*". Some raise the hand and say, "Hi", or "Hello". In the Armed Forces and the police, it is customary to raise the right hand to salute to the national flag and the superiors. A handshake is a common form of greeting in many parts of the world. The custom of shaking hands varies from one nation to another and also from one culture to another.

Many schools give special emphasis to the handshake. Women working in a man's world also shake hands but not the same way as men do. When one woman meets another they may not shake hands but exchange greetings by holding hands with a facial expression of joy.

Much can be understood from the way a person shakes hands. A firm handshake is a greeting between two equals. A flaccid hand indicates a weak person. Perspiring hands indicate a nervous temperament. Politicians and public people shake hands with the right hand and cup it with the left hand to convey expression of being close and concerned. Those who are close shake hands and also hold the right shoulder with the left hand. Some embrace. It is not sufficient to rely only upon the handshake to read body language. Do it simultaneously with reading of the facial expression.

> **Think it over...**
>
> Other parts of the body assist the speaker but the hands speak themselves. By them we ask, promise, invoke, dismiss, threaten, entreat, deprecate. By them we express fear, joy, grief, our doubts, assent or penitence; we show moderation or profusion, and mark number and time.
>
> — *Quintilian*

GESTURES USING THE HANDS

To express the universal gesture of complete surrender people raise the hands to show that they are not armed and mean no harm. Equally expressive is the waving of a white banner or cloth expressing the desire for non-violence.

Folded arms across the chest are a common sight all over the world. These express a position of defence. Both men and women use this gesture. Women fold their arms at a lower level because of the structure of the upper torso. The young use this gesture to defy the parents. Teachers, doctors and other professionals use it against their colleagues. Each seems to say: "I know what is best. I won't move." In the extreme, the folded arms may have clenched fists. This gesture encourages others to become equally rigid and not change their views. This is a common sight when two parties debate upon an issue.

In the process of a conversation or a negotiation, the purpose should be to help people open up, and not 'turn off'. If this is not done, the negotiation can fail totally. It would only be a waste of time. A person on the defensive does not listen. Even if he does physically, he is not receiving the message because he has his mental doors shut. He is therefore not a part of the communication process.

To counter the position, encourage the person to open up. This is possible when there is an amendment in the offer. Some concessions are allowed. A few additional benefits are announced. It is also possible when an altogether new offer is opened for consideration. The use of these techniques carries forward the process of communication. Some patience and tact can make it effective.

Another use of hands is when a person tightly holds on to the arms of the chair he is sitting on or folds his arms to clench the upper arm tightly. This sight is common during interviews and on flights when a person is nervous.

When a person holds the hands on the hips, the gesture indicates readiness. This is a common sight amongst sportsmen. When people adopt and follow goals, it is usual to see the person with the hands on the hips and legs apart, giving instructions to achieve what one has set for. Sometimes, young people adopt this gesture to face their parents.

The gesture of standing with arms widespread on a table indicates an ultimatum. This may come from a young person who does not approve the parents' demands or from a subordinate, who is talking to the boss to retaliate unreasonable demands. One needs to handle such situations with patience. One could hear the complaint smilingly, reassuring the person that perhaps he is not aware of the complete facts.

Hands joined together at the back and the chin pushed up indicates over-confidence, or even defiance. Policewomen use this gesture often. However, girls are taught not to have their hands behind the back as it places emphasis on the bosom, which is not approved by many cultures.

When a person rests the elbow on the table and places the hand to cover the mouth, it means that the person is holding back something. It also reflects self-doubt and lying. In conversation, it means holding back the words. This can also mean that the person is holding back the negotiation to come to a conclusion. A sudden covering of the mouth with the hand means astonishment.

Everyone is acquainted with gesticulating movements made by public speakers. These aim at emphasizing what they speak. Politicians use the pointed finger often. It is intended to show direction. For still greater emphasis some people use the fist. It is primarily a masculine gesture and used to express anger and hostility. It can provoke the other person to follow. Public speakers use this gesture to emphasize firm determination, a declaration or a desperate vow. Some use it as a means of defiance.

Palm at the back of the neck is a defensive gesture used frequently by children. Some adults use it too. Women use it deceptively when they pretend to do up their hair. It reflects what is popularly referred to as a 'pain in the neck'.

Women move their hand slowly to feel the pendant. This is a reassuring gesture. In the same way, men may indulge in hand-pinching, feeling the fleshy part of the hand, putting the pencil in the mouth or feeling the chair before sitting on it. These are re-assuring gestures. Such people seek help and co-operation.

Couples hold hands or arms and even lean upon each other to express the right of possession or ownership. Some place the arms around the waist or the shoulders. These gestures reflect intimacy.

Placing the fingertips together with the elbows resting on the table indicates confidence, leaning towards being smug, an egoist and proud. One often sees the businessmen, lawyers and teachers using these gestures. These people feel that they are important. This is a common sight when one party feels more important on the negotiating table.

Drumming on the table or the handle of the chair or tapping of the toe or the heel on the floor, indicate that the person is seeking re-assurance. This beat is likened to the heartbeat of the mother when the baby is in the womb. The rhythmic beat also indicates boredom. When the beat slows down, it expresses reconsideration whether one should accept an offer, or not. Thoughtless scribbling and drawing absentmindedly also indicate boredom.

SITTING GESTURES

One can learn much by observing how people behave when sitting. On entering a room people look for a chair that is in harmony with their temperament. Sitting on a higher chair reflects dominance. Judges always sit on elevated chairs. It puts them in a position of advantage. In many games, the umpires occupy high seats. If all the chairs are at the same level, people still look for special positions.

People adopt all kinds of postures to sit when talking to people across the table. People sit on the edge of the chair, bending forward, supporting the cheek with the hand and elbow resting on the table. Some sit relaxed on the chair. They have a smile on the face and their feet rest comfortably on the floor. Others sit leaning forward with the right elbow resting on the armrest, and the palm supporting the chin with the index finger on the cheek and eyes on the person sitting across.

Sitting postures can be positive or negative. The positive person is eager to communicate and complete a deal. On the other hand, the negative person is physically present but is suspicious and secretive. He will have his arms and legs crossed in a defensive gesture, may have the head tilted forward and will look above his spectacles to evaluate the situation. If he looks at the door, or shifts the body and has feet turned towards the door, he is probably waiting to leave. His facial expression may give him away when he gives 'a crooked smile', or may give 'a cold shoulder', or may 'glance sideways'.

The more important the person sitting, the greater the evaluation he will carry out. Some evaluate critically. Others adopt a positive attitude. The rest adopt a wait-and-see attitude, depending upon actual performance.

THE LEGS

One does not pay as much attention to the legs as much as to the hands and arms, but they are as expressive about the feelings and emotions of a person.

When a person stands straight and erect with a calm face, it indicates confidence. An erect posture is a sign of self-assurance. Straight back and square shoulders exude confidence.

Like the arms, crossed legs too indicate a defensive posture. People adopt different styles of crossing legs. Most people have the right leg crossing over the left leg. Some, particularly Americans, have the left leg over the right leg forming the figure "4". When negotiating, if one of the parties has the legs crossed, it is difficult to come to a conclusion. When a person is sitting alone and has his legs crossed, it means he is bored. This is a common sight at the airport or the railway station, for the persons waiting for a flight or train. Even in the office, a person waiting for an appointment may have his legs crossed.

A person sitting with the leg on the armrest may look comfortable, but the gesture indicates that he is an uncooperative person who could not be bothered with what is being discussed. His indifference to the situation is visible. Some times purchase managers use this gesture against salesmen, who need to change their approach. Another variation of this gesture is when a person sits with the feet on the table or another chair. He may also sit backwards, using the back of the chair as a shield. These gestures reflect dominance and an aggressive attitude.

WALKING GESTURES

Every person has a walking style that can easily be recognized by friends and acquaintances. However, we cannot overlook that emotions continue to influence the walking gestures unconsciously adopted by people.

Persons who adopt and pursue goals sincerely walk rapidly with a swing in their arms. The secretive persons walk with the hands in the pockets. They criticize freely and run people down.

Persons who are dejected and frustrated walk with their heads down, looking ahead only sometimes. The shoulders of such people are stooped. They have their hands in the pockets. People who are pre-occupied with problems also walk with their head down. They have the hands behind their back.

When you see a person walking with his head high, moving at a calculated, impressive pace with a swing in the arms, rest assured he is a pompous person, who thinks much of himself.

It is not uncommon to see people pacing up and down, invariably in deep thought, looking for an answer to a difficult problem. They walk with the head down and hands behind the back. It is best not to interrupt or disturb such people. This can break the flow of thoughts and irritate them.

Sometimes, one watches people walking closely, speaking softly in confidence and gradually placing an arm on the shoulder. This gesture indicates an aggressive readiness to dominate the person spoken to.

When walking, kicking the ground or an imaginary object indicates irritation, anger or frustration. Kicking on the door is a similar gesture.

> **Think it over...**
>
> The art of walking is at once suggestive of the dignity of man. – Progressive motion alone implies power, but in almost every other instance it seems a power gained at the expense of self-possession.
>
> — *Tuckerman*

MOVING CLOSER

It is not unusual to see a person moving closer to the other when talking. This is a common sight amongst dating couples. Even during business negotiations the persons may move closer to express shared confidence. One person always initiates the move. If the other person continues to remain seated or standing in the same place, it means that mutual confidence is growing between them. However, if the other person retaliates by moving away, it indicates that the person is 'turned off' and is not ready for a closer relationship.

SPECIAL GESTURES

In the foregoing pages we have discussed body gestures pertaining to the face, parts of the face, the head, the arms, hands and the legs. These have been discussed individually for easy comprehension. However, a human being is a composite being. A person reacts as a whole. It is not that some gestures are more prominent and understandable than others. Only a continued observation and study can enable a person to understand body language.

When people visit they are formally dressed. A gentleman would be dressed in a coat and pant, and may have a necktie to match. In an office, he would do his work and go back. However, if he were on a visit to your house, he would sit all dressed until he feels welcome and at ease. Unbuttoning the coat indicates the beginning of an opening process. Taking off the coat would be a step ahead. When he lets go the formal set-up, he will take off the necktie and feel comfortable. He may also fold up the sleeves. Finally, one is completely at ease when one takes off the shoes, as is customary in some homes.

Many people fidget in their chairs. It is common to see school children doing it. People fidget when they are tired or not interested in what is going on. They are also restless when the furniture is uncomfortable or the environment is oppressive and they are eager to leave because their mind is elsewhere. In general, fidgety behaviour indicates nervousness. It must be handled patiently because the person could be totally 'turned off'. When you realise that a person's gestures indicate that he is nervous, do not act aggressively. Instead, be patient and try to make the person comfortable. Ask if you could help in any way.

Even during an interview one gets to observe signals of nervousness. The person may hold the handles of the chair tightly or the hands may be clenched. The hand-wringing gesture indicates that the person is sitting on the hot seat trying to answer very difficult questions.

Mucous tends to choke the throat when a person is anxious or nervous. This makes it necessary to clear the throat before speaking. Men clear the throat more than women. Children do it the least. Some prefer to drink a few sips of water before they speak. A hot cup of tea or coffee also helps keep the throat clear. Whistling is yet another gesture that indicates apprehension and anxiety.

OBSERVING SELF-CONTROL

When anxious, it is natural for a person to try to observe self-control. One can get to observe typical cases during interviews. People are just as nervous when visiting a dentist. The person gives an impression as though he or she is holding back from visiting a toilet. He will hold the handle of the chair tightly and have the ankles locked. If he is not holding the chair handles, he may have the hands behind the back holding the wrist or clenching the fists. One can 'see' the effort to remain calm and maintain self-control.

POINTS TO PONDER

1. An understanding of body language is as important as the knowledge of the spoken and written languages.
2. Sign language and body language is not the same thing.
3. One begins to learn body language only through keen observation.
4. After observation, the gestures must be analyzed to get their meaning.
5. Facial expressions are the key to understanding body language.
6. A smile is the easiest way to improve one's looks.
7. Smoking habit leaves behind telltale marks about the smoker.

8. Eyes succinctly express more about a person than any other part of the body.
9. The use and handling of spectacles have their own stories to tell.
10. Every part of the face has something special to communicate.
11. The use of the hands expresses the most about a person.
12. The knowledge of sitting gestures helps understand a person better.
13. Legs are just as expressive about the feelings and emotions of a person as are the hands.
14. The walking style differentiates one person from another.
15. Body gestures are best observed as a whole.

Self-appraisal of Communication Skills

Everyone believes that he or she can communicate well. However, facts reveal that it is not true. Very few people possess good communication skills. Most people just pass through life making the best of what comes their way.

Everyday life is constituted of a variety of activities. Our success is related to a large degree to our communication skills in relation to these activities. At times, we need to communicate verbally. On other occasions, we use the written word. At the same time, our body keeps communicating a lot of information. Sometimes we are aware of it. Many times we are not. We communicate in accordance with the prevalent situation and our own perception of communication needs. We also react in harmony with our perception of what is right or wrong. This can result in a lot of wasted effort. Therefore, it becomes essential to look at various situations within home, the workplace and in the community where we need to communicate. To distinguish between the variety of situations most of us face every day, the activities have been treated separately.

To carry out a realistic self-appraisal, it is necessary that you should mark your response to each of the statements honestly. You can fill in the responses in privacy and need not share them with anyone. They are only for your personal use. They will help you understand your own strengths and limitations. For your convenience, all the questionnaires have been prepared in the same way, and you need to mark them using the same criteria. If your response to a statement is **never**, you should tick or circle 1. If it is **sometimes**, you should mark 2. If your response is **usually**, mark 3 and if it is **always**, mark 4.

PERSONAL SELF-APPRAISAL

One must begin with the self. What kind of an image do you project of yourself in everyday life? Much will depend upon your personality and your attitudes about personal grooming, care and clothes. When you are conscious about yourself, you communicate a positive image. Listed below are common everyday situations. Mark your responses by ticking or encircling the appropriate number.

1. I am very conscious and give complete attention to personal grooming. 1 2 3 4
2. I shave every day, or 1 2 3 4

   I sport a beard, which is maintained on a regular basis.
3. I have a haircut and manicure at regular periods. 1 2 3 4
4. I wear clean clothes that are always well ironed. 1 2 3 4
5. I believe that good habits lead to an attractive personality. 1 2 3 4
6. I seek to update my knowledge regularly. 1 2 3 4

7. I believe that continuous self-improvement is the foundation of a successful life. 1 2 3 4
8. I read the newspaper everyday. 1 2 3 4
9. I read at least 12 books every year. 1 2 3 4
10. I have an optimistic attitude towards life. 1 2 3 4
11. I believe that a smile helps open the door wherever one goes. 1 2 3 4
12. I remain composed when asked to speak in public. 1 2 3 4
13. I maintain self-control when provoked. 1 2 3 4
14. Etiquette and good manners make life easy for everyone. 1 2 3 4
15. I listen more than what I speak. 1 2 3 4

Add up all the numbers that you have ticked. If the total is 30, or less, you need to pay special attention to the image you project of you. If the total is between 31 and 45, you have positive habits but need to strengthen those areas where you have scored less. 46 and above indicates that you are in control. You are communicating well through your personality.

Think it over...

Man must build his culture about the complete human personality...Whatever nourishes the personality, humanizes it, refines it, deepens it, intensifies its aptitude and broadens its field of action is good; whatever limits it or thwarts it, whatever sends it back into tribal patterns and limits its capacity for human co-operation and communion must be counted as bad.

— *Lewis Mumford*

COMMUNICATING WITH THE SELF

Before one can communicate effectively with others it is important that one must be able to communicate effectively with the self. How well do you communicate with your inner-self? Listed below are situations that can guide you in this direction. Mark your responses by ticking or encircling the appropriate number.

1.	I believe in God and the love He showers upon everyone without distinction.	1	2	3	4
2.	I see the manifestation of God in all forms of life and objects.	1	2	3	4
3.	I find great solace and power in prayer.	1	2	3	4
4.	I spend a few minutes in silent introspection everyday.	1	2	3	4
5.	Many of my problems get solved when I sit quietly searching for answers from within.	1	2	3	4

Add up all the numbers that you have ticked. If the total is 10, or less, you need to pay special attention to your communication with the self. If the total is between 11 and 15, you have good habits but can strengthen those areas where you have scored less. 16 and above indicates that you are in control. Communicate with the self to understand yourself better and get ahead in life.

READING SKILLS

Reading is the first step to becoming knowledgeable. Reading, which aims at understanding and interpretation of information, leads one to study. Studying aims at detailed investigation and analysis of a subject or situation. This eventually leads one to be learned and knowledgeable. Unfortunately, most people are not fond of reading. Much of the reading is imposed upon people by their individual circumstances. How are your reading skills? Listed below are situations that can guide you in this direction. Mark your responses by ticking or encircling the appropriate number.

1.	I am fond of reading.	1 2 3 4
2.	I read with a purpose in mind.	1 2 3 4
3.	For easy comprehension I try to figure out how the book I am reading is structured.	1 2 3 4
4.	I adjust my reading to the type of reading material.	1 2 3 4
5.	I read so that I can learn more in less time.	1 2 3 4

Add up all the numbers that you have ticked. If the total is 10, or less, you need to pay special attention to your reading skills. If the total is between 11 and 15, you have good reading habits but can strengthen those areas where you have scored less. 16 and above indicates that you are in control. Good reading habits will help you learn how to communicate effectively.

Think it over...

When I am reading a book, whether wise or silly, it seems to be alive and talking to me.

— *Jonathan Swift*

LISTENING SKILLS

Are you a good listener? For effective communication it is essential that before one can speak or write well, one must be able to listen well. Children who are unable to hear because of defects at birth are unable to learn how to speak. This also affects their writing skills. Most of us are not good listeners. This may seem hard to believe but it is true. Listed below are situations that can guide you in this direction. Mark your responses by ticking or encircling the appropriate number.

1. As a child I was attentive in school and later at college. 1 2 3 4
2. I do not receive complaints that I do not listen to people talking to me. 1 2 3 4
3. If I do not understand what is being said I repeat what I have understood, and seek confirmation. 1 2 3 4
4. My mind does not go astray when someone is speaking to me. 1 2 3 4
5. Unless it is required, I never interrupt when someone is speaking to me. 1 2 3 4

Add up all the numbers that you have ticked. If the total is 10 or less, you need to pay special attention to your listening habits. If the total is between 11 and 15, you have good listening habits but can strengthen those areas where you have scored less. 16 and above indicates that you are in control. Good listening habits will help you learn how to communicate effectively.

USING THE TELEPHONE

When Graham Bell gave telephone to the world, he could not have imagined that one day it would change the way people think or work. He could also have never imagined that some day the telephone would become a sophisticated instrument, to be found not only in offices but also in every room of the house. The modern generation cannot think of a life without telephone. At the touch of a button, it is now possible to talk to friends and relatives anywhere in the world.

Each day, as the telecommunication companies push the tariffs down, people are encouraged to speak more on the telephone. Everything spoken on the telephone may not be productive. Everyone is also not acquainted with the correct use of this useful gadget. Thus the effectiveness of the communication is affected. How do you rate yourself for speaking effectively on the telephone? Listed below are common everyday situations we come across. Mark your responses by ticking or encircling the appropriate number.

1.	I use the telephone only when I know it will increase my effectiveness.	1 2 3 4
2.	When I get through, the first thing I do is to disclose my name with a smile.	1 2 3 4
3.	When I am connected to the person I wish to talk to, I courteously explain the purpose of the call.	1 2 3 4
4.	I ensure that the conversation is clear, concise and to the point.	1 2 3 4
5.	If I need to provide time-consuming information, I tell the caller that I will revert back later. I do so when free.	1 2 3 4

Add up all the numbers that you have ticked. If the total is 10 or less, you need to pay special attention to your use of the telephone. If the total is between 11 and 15, you have good habits but can strengthen those areas where you have scored less. 16 and above indicates that you are in control. Communicate on the telephone to be effective.

MOBILE PHONES

More than the conventional telephones fitted at homes and offices, the mobile phones have revolutionised life when we find everyone using them. These phones have undoubtedly increased productivity and brought people closer. However, with added facilities and lower tariffs, people, particularly the younger generation, is going overboard. More time is being spent on the mobile phones than is necessary. Are you using mobile phones to your advantage?

1. I do not give my mobile number to everyone. 1 2 3 4
2. I speak as courteously on the mobile phone as I do on the regular phone. 1 2 3 4
3. I use the mobile phone only when I am away from home or office. 1 2 3 4
4. When driving, I always stop the vehicle before responding to a call. 1 2 3 4
5. As far as practical, I limit my calls on the mobile. 1 2 3 4

Add up all the numbers that you have ticked. If the total is 10 or less, you need to pay special attention to your use of the mobile phone. If the total is between 11 and 15, you have good habits but can strengthen those areas where you have scored less. 16 and above indicates that you are in control. Communicate to the best of your ability.

COMMUNICATING WITH THE SPOUSE

Your relationship with the spouse depends upon how well both of you can communicate. When communications become weak, differences begin to raise their ugly heads.

Listed below are common situations that we see everyday. Mark you responses by ticking or encircling the appropriate number.

1. I believe love is selfless caring for one another. 1 2 3 4
2. Good marriages are based upon personal commitment to each other. 1 2 3 4
3. Strong marital relationships are built upon good communication and understanding in the couple. 1 2 3 4
4. Communication between a married couple is strong when both the partners express their views and feelings unhesitatingly. 1 2 3 4
5. Silence, or a breakdown of communication between a couple is a sure sign of a deteriorating marital relationship. 1 2 3 4
6. My spouse and I accept that the children and the home are our joint responsibility. 1 2 3 4
7. I never let down or speak against my spouse's family. 1 2 3 4
8. I never unduly praise my own family. 1 2 3 4
9. Whenever my spouse and I feel strongly about something, we sit down and talk about it. 1 2 3 4
10. My spouse and I go out for an outing by ourselves at least once every month. 1 2 3 4

Add up all the numbers that you have ticked. If the total is 20 or less, you need to pay special attention to your relationship with the spouse. If the total is between 21 and 30, you enjoy a good relationship with the spouse, but need to strengthen the areas where you have scored less. 31 and above indicates that you are in control. You can be proud of good communications between you and the spouse.

COMMUNICATING WITH THE CHILDREN

Next to the spouse, it is equally important that one must have good relationship with one's children. Both the husband and the wife are responsible towards the children. However, one must ensure that an individual is able to communicate well so that the children may not drift away. Listed below are common situations that we see everyday. Mark you responses by ticking or encircling the appropriate number.

1. My children and I enjoy a friendly relationship. 1 2 3 4
2. Whenever invited, I participate in my children's school or college programmes. 1 2 3 4
3. Our family always eats together at dinnertime. 1 2 3 4
4. I accept that every child is born unique, and must be treated accordingly. 1 2 3 4
5. Generation gap is a term used to cover up poor communications between two generations. 1 2 3 4

Add up all the numbers that you have ticked. If the total is 10 or less, you need to pay special attention to the communication between you and the children. If the total is between 11 and 15, you communicate well with the children, but can strengthen those areas where you have scored less. 16 and above indicates that you are in control. Keep up with your efforts to communicate well with the children.

> **Think it over...**
>
> The first duty to children is to make them happy. — If you have made them so, you have wronged them. — No other good they may get can make up for that.
>
> — *Buxton*

COMMUNICATING AT THE WORKPLACE

Perhaps at no other place are the communicating skills put to test more than at the workplace. Depending upon the responsibilities one is entrusted with, one needs to be good at verbal communication; must possess good writing skills and be able to make good presentations. One also communicates non-verbally through body language, many times without being conscious about it. Since the ultimate success one achieves is largely dependant upon an individual's communication skills, it is necessary that one must go through self-appraisal of various activities that are common at the workplace.

COMMUNICATING THROUGH LETTERS

The most popular form of communication at the national and international level is through letters. Even in everyday life, letters play an important part in helping maintain relationships. Some write very good letters. One enjoys going through the letter repeatedly. It not only conveys information, it also touches the heart. It is for this reason that young couples preserve what they refer to as 'love letters'. Listed below are everyday situations that we see. Mark your responses by ticking or encircling the appropriate number.

1. I am usually complimented for a neat and legible handwriting. 1 2 3 4
2. I always write neatly to ensure that the reader does not find it difficult to read. 1 2 3 4
3. When I write a letter, I write as though the letter is my personal messenger. 1 2 3 4
4. My letters are effective. They achieve the purpose of writing them. 1 2 3 4
5. I always put in my best effort to write a letter. 1 2 3 4

Add up all the numbers that you have ticked. If the total is 10 or less, you need to pay special attention to the letters you write. If the total is between 11 and 15, you write fairly good letters but can strengthen those areas where you have scored less. 16 and above indicates that you are in control. Keep up with your efforts to communicate well through letters.

WRITING MEMOS

Writing memos is a common practice followed for inter-office communication. Memos do away with the formal aspects of writing letters. They can be direct and to the point. Despite this directness, memos too fail to communicate the correct message and can be misinterpreted, and fail to achieve their purpose. It is therefore necessary that care must be taken in using this medium of communication effectively. Listed below are common everyday situations that we see. Mark your responses by ticking or encircling the appropriate number.

1. I write memos only when I think it is necessary for the intended purpose. 1 2 3 4

2. I ensure that the memo is clear, concise and easy to understand. 1 2 3 4
3. I seek a response to get a feedback that the memo is clearly understood. 1 2 3 4
4. When writing a memo I ensure that the wordings project a positive attitude towards the work at hand. 1 2 3 4
5. I always follow up on the action that is desired in the memo. 1 2 3 4

Add up all the numbers that you have ticked. If the total is 10 or less, you need to pay special attention to the memos you write. If the total is between 11 and 15, you write fairly good memos but can strengthen those areas where you have scored less. 16 and above indicates that you are in control. Keep up with your efforts to communicate well through memos.

> **Think it over...**
>
> A writer is dear and necessary to us in the measure in which he reveals to us the inner working of his soul.
>
> — *Leo Tolstoy*

OFFICE REPORTS

It is usual for the management to seek reports on different aspects of the working of organisations. Unlike memos, reports need to have a formal layout with facts and figures. Memos attract immediate attention and action. Reports are usually intended to be tools for introspection and long-term planning. They need a serious, though practical approach; and also a good control over the language and writing skills. Listed below are everyday situations that we see. Mark your responses by ticking or encircling the appropriate number.

1.	I ensure that the report is based upon facts, and not hearsay.	1	2	3	4
2.	I agree that it is not the quantum but the quality of information that is important in a report.	1	2	3	4
3.	I collect the data, write the report and then revise it several times before I finalise it.	1	2	3	4
4.	Whenever possible, I include figures, illustrations and photographs in a report.	1	2	3	4
5.	I ensure that the best language skills are used in preparing a report.	1	2	3	4
6.	I ensure that the report is clear, concise and correct.	1	2	3	4
7.	I always highlight important facts by using bold type, wherever necessary.	1	2	3	4
8.	Whenever a problem is listed in the report, I also include possible solutions to correct the situation.	1	2	3	4
9.	On the first page of the report I include an appropriate title, explain the purpose of the report and also give the source of the facts and individuals consulted.	1	2	3	4
10.	I ensure that the report is correctly typed, and the sheets are bound, or placed in a file or folder for presentation.	1	2	3	4

Add up all the numbers that you have ticked. If the total is 20 or less, you need to pay special attention to the preparation of reports. If the total is between 21 and 30, you are already writing reasonably good reports but need to strengthen the areas where you have scored less. 31 and above indicates that you are in control. You can be proud of your ability to communicate well through the reports you compile and write.

E-MAIL MESSAGES

It has become commonplace to communicate through e-mail. It is swifter and effective if both the sender and the recipient open their mailboxes everyday. Besides it is very cost effective. E-mail has opened the world to everyone, making international communication swift and easy. How does e-mail affect your functioning every day? Listed below are everyday situations that we see. Mark your responses by ticking or encircling the appropriate number.

1.	I read my email at a fixed time each day.	1	2	3	4
2.	I respond to the mail immediately after reading it or forward it, if necessary.	1	2	3	4
3.	I keep the email on my computer for some time in case I need to refer to it later.	1	2	3	4
4.	I delete unnecessary e-mails immediately on receiving them.	1	2	3	4
5.	I clear up my computer of all old mail every three months.	1	2	3	4

Add up all the numbers that you have ticked. If the total is 10 or less, you need to give more attention to your use of email. If the total is between 11 and 15, you are aware of the problem but can strengthen those areas where you have scored less. 16 and above indicates that you are in control. Continue to use email to add to your effectiveness.

MEETINGS

Effective meetings require both good communication skills and time management. Many meetings fail to achieve their expected goals. Therefore, one must review how effective the meetings are. How do you fare in this field? Listed below are everyday situations that we come across. Mark your responses by ticking or encircling the appropriate number.

1. I call a meeting only when it is necessary. 1 2 3 4
2. I ensure that the meeting agenda reaches the participants in time. 1 2 3 4
3. I always reach the meetings in time. 1 2 3 4
4. I always carry the complete background material to the meeting. 1 2 3 4
5. I ensure that the meeting starts on time. 1 2 3 4
6. I ensure that all the participants get an opportunity to speak. 1 2 3 4
7. I do not get angry if any of the participants disagree with me. 1 2 3 4
8. I insist that the participants must address the chair and not speak with each other. 1 2 3 4
9. I always try that the meeting must achieve the purpose it is called for. 1 2 3 4
10. I always end a meeting on time. 1 2 3 4

Add up all the numbers that you have ticked. If the total is 20 or less, you need to be more careful how you handle meetings presently. If the total is between 21 and 30, you are aware of the problem but can strengthen those areas where you have scored less. 31 and above indicates that you are in control. Meetings can be an effective way to convey your message to a lot of people.

SPEAKING SKILLS

The ability to speak well to a group of people in the office or otherwise, is a quality that is always admired. Not many people can do it convincingly. Persons who desire to get ahead at the workplace will do well to hone their public speaking skills to rise in their positions. Listed below are common everyday situations that we see. Mark your responses by ticking or encircling the appropriate number.

1. I remain composed when invited to speak to a group of people. 1 2 3 4
2. If informed in advance, I prepare myself to speak on the subject. 1 2 3 4
3. I look at the audience when speaking to them. 1 2 3 4
4. While speaking, I focus my words at the subject or problem at hand. 1 2 3 4
5. I always speak within the time allocated to me. 1 2 3 4

Add up all the numbers that you have ticked. If the total is 10 or less, you need to pay special attention to your public speaking skills. If the total is between 11 and 15, you are already doing fairly well, but can strengthen those areas where you have scored less. 16 and above indicates that you are in control. Keep up with your efforts to communicate well through public speaking skills.

Think it over...

Discretion of speech is more than eloquence; and to speak agreeably to him, with whom we deal is more than to speak in good words, or in good order.

— *Bacon*

MAKING FORMAL PRESENTATIONS

People with good communication skills are often

asked to make presentations to highlight problems, offer special bargains, or to educate and motivate the staff. With great advance in information technology, overhead projectors and slide projectors have given way to LCD projectors that can be connected to a laptop, and a wealth of information passed attractively packaged in a presentation. How do you rate yourself for such presentations? Listed below are common everyday situations that we see. Mark your responses by ticking or encircling the appropriate number.

1. I prepare my presentations well in advance.	1	2	3	4
2. I practise with my presentation until I am confident about it.	1	2	3	4
3. My presentations always have a specific goal to achieve.	1	2	3	4
4. I always follow a presentation with a question and answer session.	1	2	3	4
5. I ensure that the purpose of the presentation is achieved.	1	2	3	4

Add up all the numbers that you have ticked. If the total is 10 or less, you need to pay special attention to your presentation skills. If the total is between 11 and 15, you are already making fairly good presentations but can strengthen those areas where you have scored less. 16 and above indicates that you are in control. Keep up with your efforts to communicate well through good presentations.

COMMUNICATING AT COMMUNITY LEVEL

Man is a social being and cannot live an isolated life. Everyday we come across and deal with many people like the liftman in the building, the gardener, the watchman, taxi drivers, bus conductors, and the salesmen in the shops. We need to communicate with them. If our communication is effective, we get a better service. This way we promote happiness and feel content. Listed below are everyday situations that we come across. Mark your responses by ticking or encircling the appropriate number.

1. I always thank shop assistants, taxi drivers, the liftman and the watchman for the services they render. 1 2 3 4
2. I never hesitate to say "sorry" when I make a mistake, or cause inconvenience to someone. 1 2 3 4
3. I always lend a willing ear to those who are in trouble and seek help. 1 2 3 4
4. I believe that thoughtfulness of others is the best religion to follow. 1 2 3 4
5. I follow a policy of "live and let live" in my relationships with people. 1 2 3 4

Add up all the numbers that you have ticked. If the total is 10 or less, you need to pay special attention to your communication at the community level. If the total is between 11 and 15, you are already maintaining good relationships but can strengthen those areas where you have scored less. 16 and above indicates that you are in control. Keep up with your efforts to communicate well at the community level.

YOUR STRENGTHS AND WEAKNESSES

As you look back at the scores of different aspects of your life, you will begin to appreciate the areas of your strength and also where you need to improve your effectiveness. You should make a list of both your strengths and weaknesses. In the next step, we will discuss how you can develop your communication skills in different fields of activity.

POINTS TO PONDER

1. Very few people possess good communication skills.
2. A self-appraisal must begin with knowledge of personal strengths and weaknesses.
3. One must first be able to communicate with the self before communicating with others.
4. Good reading skills help one to become knowledgeable.
5. If one cannot listen well, one cannot communicate effectively.
6. The correct use of the telephone can add to a person's effectiveness.
7. Effective communication with the spouse is essential for peace and harmony at home.
8. When parents communicate effectively with the children, the generation gap is automatically bridged.
9. The ability to write well adds effectiveness at the workplace.
10. Without good communication skills meetings can fail.
11. Good speaking skills help a person rise above others.
12. Only a few skilled persons can make a fine presentation.
13. Good communications skills help make life easy and comfortable in the community.
14. The knowledge of your strengths and weaknesses will help you to get ahead.

Developing Communication Skills

How do you feel after you have gone through the process of self-appraisal? Are you able to appreciate your areas of strength and weakness? Are you now able to understand how communication skills affect you in everyday life at home, at the workplace and in the society?

The purpose of this exercise is to make you aware, how effective communication contributes to make a person successful. You will also notice that most of the skills required can be acquired through learning and effort. Nobody is born a good communicator. At best, one is born with instinctive communication abilities. These need to be honed. A good general educational level of the family helps the individuals to develop good skills. Personal confidence plays an important role. The important thing is to be able to convey your message to the person who can help you achieve what you want. This is possible only when you are able to develop the necessary skills and abilities.

EVERYONE IS DIFFERENT

Have you ever realised that you are a unique person? There never was one like you before you came to this world nor is there one like you today and there will never be one like you in the future. It is the combination of the many unique characteristics in you that make you what you are – a very special person!

Being unique does not mean to have nothing in common with each other. It only means that every individual reacts differently to given circumstances. Otherwise, the traits of human beings are similar. God has given everyone the choice to accept whatever one likes and reject what one does not like. It is this choice that makes some people capable and effective and the others just live ordinary lives. You are also free to choose whatever kind of life you wish to live. What we learn from our parents, teachers, friends and relatives makes us different. Every individual makes his or her choice. Nature or God do not in any way compel you to choose one way of life or another.

How do your choices help shape your life? This is possible because of your actions based upon your choices. With repeated actions one develops habits and individuals are often distinguished because of their habits, good or bad.

CHECK YOUR HABITS

You are known by the kind of habits that you have. When good habits predominate, one is known as a good person. In the same way, when bad habits are conspicuous, a person is obviously avoided. Good habits are important to individuals who want to get ahead in life.

Effective reading and comprehension, speaking, writing and in general, communicating at home, at the workplace and society are desirable habits that everyone cherishes and desires. Therefore, a person's immediate concern is to develop the skills and abilities that make a person a good communicator. Some learn this early in school; others do not realise the importance of effective communication until they experience the lack of it.

Habits are not formed overnight. They are the result of repeated actions day after day. With each repeated action, an activity gets ingrained into the human subconscious to become a habit. Every habit has its foundation in a thought. Through this thought, one visualizes what one wishes to do. The visuals motivate one to action. When actions are repeated, it becomes a habit.

The purpose of going to school and college is to learn a variety of subjects that touch everyday life. This study, in turn, prepares us to understand life better through effective communication. However, as adults, most people forget the basic lessons learnt at school and do not use the skills to their advantage. It is unfortunate that one becomes careless and fails to overlook simple skills and abilities. Learning effective communication can be as easy as going back to your school and college days and inculcate the little things like being attentive, observant and listening carefully; and practicing concentration to comprehend what is going around and be able to practice effective communication in everyday adult life.

Think it over...

Habits work more constantly and with greater force than reason, which when we have most need of it, is seldom fairly consulted and more rarely obeyed.

— *John Locke*

ATTENTIVENESS

When you are not attentive to a person speaking to you, it means that you are not listening. You may be physically present. You may also be aware that someone is talking to you. However, whatever is being spoken falls into deaf ears. This is more common than many of us would be willing to believe. Poor listening means ineffective incoming communication. When a person fails to receive the complete message, he is bound to give poor results.

Even in everyday life people do not listen attentively. People listen but without being attentive they fail to understand what has been spoken to them. The lack of attentiveness results in poor communication at home, at the workplace and in the society. People who have goals to achieve must appreciate this important fact. Do not let lack of attentiveness be a cause of failure.

GETTING THE COMPLETE MESSAGE

When listening, most people fail to get the complete message. Ask your family and friends. They will tell you that you are absent-minded. It is very much like not being attentive in the class. Listening is an acquired skill. It requires one to concentrate on what is being said.

The ability to get the full message depends upon how important the message is to the person. If it is important, one ensures that he or she does not miss out on the details. However, if it pertains to what someone else expects one to do, we fail to be attentive. The message we receive is incomplete. If one were to write the message, in all likelihood it would only be one-fourth correct.

CONFIRMING THE MESSAGE

To ensure effective communication the best thing to do is to confirm whatever is conveyed. The habit of confirming a message must be adopted when one is in school or college. If one has failed to do so, it would still be worthwhile to develop this habit at the earliest. A responsible person does not ignore the details of anything in adult life. This is possible only when the person understands what is expected when the message is passed on. It is therefore essential that one must confirm the information a person has received.

WRONG ATTITUDES

Two kinds of people inhabit this world. The vast majority looks at each other for mutual acceptance and admiration. They are literally "keeping up with the Joneses". They indulge in a variety of activities they do not like. Many of these activities make them uneasy and unhappy. However, they indulge in them saying, "What will others think about us?"

There is a smaller minority that does what is in harmony with their conscience. They could not be bothered what others think of them. They have their own beliefs and convictions, and follow their own mind. The difference between the two groups is that while one is conditioned by the negative influences of the vast majority, the smaller group stands firm, following the voice of their own conscience.

To which of these two groups do you belong? The choice is yours. Just as with other activities, this holds good about making all communication effective. It is the individual's success at stake, not that of the group. It is for the individual to ensure that he or she is correctly understood and also that an incoming message is suitably acted upon. In a group the attitudes may change. It is for individuals to develop the communication skills and abilities to get ahead in life.

> **Think it over...**
>
> People are lonely because they build walls instead of bridges.
>
> *— J. F. Newton*

MAKING A BEGINNING

The decision to communicate effectively is a positive step to improve your potential for success. It is often said: a journey of a thousand miles begins with a single step. This first step has to be a positive attitude towards all kinds of communications, spoken, written or by other means. Look at both the incoming and outgoing communications as an opportunity for success. Use each of these opportunities like rungs in a ladder that raise you to success in every field of life.

You are what you think you are. If you think you cannot do it, you will not be able to do it. With such thoughts you are inviting failure. Acquire skills and abilities to get ahead in life. Believe in yourself. Keep reminding yourself that you can do it. When things go wrong, as sometimes they do, use the mistakes as building of personal experience. After all, experience is what people learn by making mistakes. You too can add to your experience and grow.

Success is possible only when a person possesses a variety of skills and abilities. What should a person do if one does not possess some of these? There is only one way to handle this situation, and that is to acquire the skills you do not possess. Never be shy of learning. There are people who keep learning new things all the time. You too need to set out to succeed.

STEPPING TOWARDS SUCCESS

To attain your objective of communicating effectively sooner remember that success begins in the mind. Success must begin from your thoughts. You will do well to follow these simple guidelines.

- Always think of success and not failure.
- Let everyone know that you are learning to communicate effectively. Once you make your intentions public, others will remind you when you go wrong.
- Believe in yourself. You can do it if you really want to. Remind yourself of your own skills and abilities.
- Never make negative comments about yourself. This may bring you sympathy but not success.
- Set definite learning deadlines for yourself. Make plans to achieve these targets. Follow up with action.
- Let your confidence grow slowly as you attain what you set out to do. Smaller successes will lead you to bigger successes.
- Make a deliberate effort to get over your shortcomings through proper assessment, understanding the causes and correct planning and execution.

GETTING OVER LIMITATIONS

It is natural if one wants to get over one's drawbacks to be able to go ahead. Earlier, you assessed yourself on the basis of certain parameters, and checked your scores. You might have scored well in some activities, and not too well in others. If you have been honest with yourself, the scores would have guided you to your own strengths and weaknesses. Let us revise the activities and work out ways to have a balanced approach towards every aspect of life.

Personal Self-appraisal

Let us get back to the chart on personal self-appraisal. The chart serves two definite purposes. First, it is a guide that lets you know your strengths and weaknesses in this field of activity. Second, you get to know that if you adopt all the activities, you would have an attractive personality that would lead you to success. It is not enough to know merely what is right or wrong. The important thing is to know how to become successful in what you have set out to achieve. Some of the facts that emerge from this self-appraisal are:

- Attention to personal grooming is the key to developing an attractive personality.
- Do not ignore everyday needs like a shave, trimming the beard or moustaches or a periodical manicure.
- Neat and clean clothes speak loudly of a person. They add to personal confidence.
- Keep a check on your habits. Good habits enhance the personality. Bad habits will always let you down.

- Continuous self-improvement leads one to success.
- Be well informed. You must read the newspaper everyday. This will keep you updated on what is going around the world.
- Reading at least one book every month will greatly add to your knowledge. If you cannot afford to buy books, join a library.
- A smile is an easy way to improve one's looks.
- Optimism is contagious. Spread it wherever you go. People will be grateful to you for it.
- Self-control is a sign of maturity and understanding.
- Etiquette and good manners make life easy and smooth. People will remember you for it.
- There is a great shortage of listeners. They are in demand everywhere.

Think it over...

The perfection of dress is in the union of three requisites – in its being comfortable, cheap and tasteful.

— *Christian Nestell Bovee*

Communicating With the Self

If you cannot understand and communicate with yourself, you cannot possibly communicate effectively with others. Learn to observe self-control. Practise virtuous habits. Avoid sinful activities however harmless they may appear. Some of the facts that emerge from the self-appraisal are:

- The Supreme Power is the creator, sustainer and destroyer of this universe.
- God showers love on everyone without exception.
- God is manifested in all forms of life and objects.
- When nothing works, prayer does. Try it out.
- God resides within each one of us. Connect with your conscience to talk to Him. Your questions will be answered.
- When God is with you, nothing can be against you.

Reading Skills

Unfortunately, very few are fond of reading. Most people leave behind their books in school and college. This is a major cause of poor knowledge and lack of communication skills. Even in professions like medicine, engineering and law many people are shy of reading and end up with mediocrity. Some of the facts that have emerged from the self-appraisal are:

- Reading is important if one has to keep pace with the knowledge explosion.
- Good reading habits lead to effective communication.
- The reading material must lead one to personal development and growth.
- If time is a constraint the reading speed can easily be increased with a little effort.
- The reading material must be aimed at self-improvement, at increasing efficiency at the workplace and must also provide some entertainment.
- Self-study is a shortcut to personal wisdom.

Listing Skills

Effective communication is not restricted to only sending out correctly worded messages. It is equally important that one should receive and understand incoming messages. This means one must be a good listener. Very few people are good listeners. People are more comfortable with outgoing messages rather than incoming messages. Unfortunately, lack of listening skills affects one's speaking and writing skills. Some of the facts that emerge from the self-appraisal are:

- Listening skills are initially acquired at the school and college level.
- Poor listening skills affect productivity at all levels.
- One may listen and yet not comprehend what is said because of lack of attentiveness.
- An immediate feedback ensures that what was said has registered clearly.
- The mind strays into inattentiveness when one is not interested in the topic.
- Interruption breaks an otherwise good dialogue.

Using the Telephone

The telephone has changed the way people think and work. It has changed the way people communicate. It has connected the people all over the world. However, just as it has increased productivity in every sphere, it has also created problems of interruptions with the telephone ringing at the wrong time and taking away much of valuable time. It has encouraged people to speak more than necessary, stealing away time from more important tasks like planning and management. Some of the points that emerge from the self-appraisal are:

- The telephone is a great time robber.
- It has encouraged people to talk more than is necessary.
- The telephone can greatly influence productivity, both for good and bad.
- Good speaking manners are as important on the telephone as they are in normal everyday conversation.
- The telephone users must observe self-restraint to speak unnecessarily.
- To avoid wastage of valuable time, calls must be scheduled at times when one is comparatively less busy.

The Mobile Phone

The mobile phone has certainly brought people closer. Now it is possible to reach out to people away from home or vice versa. However, it has greatly increased the nuisance of people carrying mobile phones to meetings, cinema halls and other places, often ringing at the wrong time and wrong place. It is a great communication tool, but must be used with caution, ensuring that it is not a nuisance to others. Some of the points that emerge from the self-appraisal are:

- A mobile phone is a convenient device. It should not cause inconvenience to others.
- Many people wrongly believe that just because a person has a mobile phone, it gives one the right to reach out to him or her at any time.

- A person keeps a mobile for personal benefit, not to be disturbed at odd times and situations.
- One must observe the normal courtesies on the mobile phone as one does on the normal telephone.
- Use of the mobile phone while driving is a great risk to life and property.

Communicating With the Spouse

Marriage continues to be the oldest and the best institution in the world. Many efforts have been made to have alternate kinds of relationships to avoid limitations that are a part of marital relationship. However, sooner or later, one realises that substitutes are substitutes. They are not the real things. A good marital relationship is needed forever. The foundation of a good marriage is built upon effective communication between the couple. Some of the points that emerge from the self-appraisal are:

- Marriage continues to be the oldest and the finest institution in the world.
- A strong marital relationship is based upon good communication and understanding between husband and wife.
- Love means giving without any expectations.
- Doubt and hesitation to communicate are signs of a deteriorating relationship.
- Prolonged silence between couples is a sign of discord, and not of harmony.
- Children need both the father and the mother. Both must contribute towards their welfare.

- Everyone is sensitive about his or her paternal families. Marriage does not give permission to any of the partners to unduly praise or malign them.
- The best way for a couple to end differences of opinion is to sit down and talk.
- A couple must reserve some time to be on their own to open up and strengthen personal trust and commitment.

Communicating With the Children

Next to the spouse, it is the children that need attention and care. Children are human beings. Effective communication is necessary to keep the relationship alive. Since every child is an individual he or she is different and may not think the same way as the parents. It is important that special effort may be made to understand and care for them. Some of the points that have emerged from the self-appraisal are:

- Every child is born different. Treat him or her appropriately.
- A child needs both the father and the mother.
- For a child it is not enough to be only provided for. A child seeks care and personal interaction with the parents.
- A child seeks approval and appreciation, not criticism.
- A child needs to be guided and helped. This can only be done with love and tact.
- Never let the communication channel between you and the child break. It will encourage both of you to drift away from each other.

- Communication channels, once broken, are hard to mend.

Communicating Through Letters

Most people are not fond of writing letters. However, a person who needs to get ahead must know how to write a good letter because it will be necessary to write all kinds of letters in various circumstances. Letters will have to be written to the children's school, to the Municipal Corporation, to the banks and to friends and relatives. If they must achieve their purpose, they must be well written. Some of the points that have emerged from the self-appraisal are:

- Most people lack confidence and hesitate to write letters.
- A neat and legible handwriting is the foundation of an effective letter. Some have now substituted it with typewriting.
- A letter is a personal messenger of the sender to the recipient. Its effectiveness will depend upon the choice of words and presentation.
- A positive feedback confirms that the letter was effective.

> **Think it over...**
>
> Pens are most dangerous tools, more sharp by odds.
>
> Than swords, and cut more keen than whips or rods.
>
> — *John Taylor*

Writing Memos

Memo is a short form for the word: memorandum, meaning a note sent from one person to another in an organization. It also means a note recording something for future use. We are immediately concerned with the writing of notes within the organization. The notes for future use are usually formal legal documents, and are preferably drafted by legal experts. While the notes exchanged within the organization are not very formal, the documents for future use are. Many memos are exchanged in every organization, and to be effective it is necessary that a memo must fulfill the norms for writing a good document. Some of the points that have emerged from the self-appraisal are:

- A memo must be written only when necessary.
- Unless a memo is clear, concise and complete, there is a possibility that it could be misinterpreted and misunderstood.
- The positive attitude of the person writing the memo must be visible in the note.
- A feedback from the recipient ensures the effectiveness of the memo.
- A follow-up action is necessary after the memo is sent and received.

Writing Reports

In every organization it becomes necessary to prepare reports on a variety of subjects. These reports are usually used for planning purpose. It is necessary that persons who possess good writing skills and are well versed with the subject at hand write these reports. These reports are like in-house books. Several copies may be prepared and shared by the management and the personnel involved in the project. Some of the points that have emerged from the self-appraisal are:

- All reports must be based on facts.
- A report may be long or short, but it must include the facts, an analysis, forecasts and suggestions pertaining to the subject.
- Figures, graphs, illustrations and photographs enhance the value of a report.
- Clarity of thought and good writing skills helps make a report effective.
- Most reports are plain cold facts. A good presentation helps make them more attractive.
- Revision and editing make a report user-friendly.
- Ultimately, a report must be like a mini-book.
- Sufficient copies of a report must be made to reach the management and all the concerned persons.

E-mail Messages

E-mail is a good medium for sending and receiving information. It is swift. It connects a person to people and organizations around the world. It is cost effective. E-mail messages do away with the formalities of a letter. They can be short and direct. Some of the points that have emerged from the self-appraisal are:

- E-mail messages can arrive and be sent at any time of the day or night.
- The mailbox must be opened once a day at a time allocated for the purpose.

- The mail can be responded to immediately.
- Unsolicited mail should be deleted.
- The computer must be cleared of old mail periodically.

Meetings

Millions of meetings are conducted all over the world each day. Very few achieve their purpose. A common cause is poor communication skills. To ensure that this does not happen one must understand how to make a meeting effective. Just as failed meetings hinder growth and productivity, the ability to handle meetings well takes one towards success. Some of the points that have emerged from the self-appraisal are:

- Many meetings are a waste of time. They can be avoided.
- At all meetings the agenda should be the basis of discussion and action.
- Meetings must begin and end on time.
- During the meeting all the participants must be given an opportunity to speak.
- To be effective, the person presiding the meeting must remain in control.
- The participants must not talk to each other. They must address the chair.
- One should not get provoked if there is a difference of opinion amongst the participants. An effort must be made to agree on points of common interest.
- The person presiding at the meeting must remember the purpose of the meeting. The discussion should lead in that direction.

- A meeting can be said to be effective if the purpose of the meeting is achieved.

Speaking Skills

Although many people claim to possess good speaking skills, very few can really deliver well. Most of them are mediocre. Good speaking skills are an asset at the workplace and also in the society. These can be acquired through practice and effort. Some of the points that have emerged from the self-appraisal are:

- Very few people possess good speaking skills.
- Good speakers do not acquire their skills by birth. They acquire them like any other skill and ability.
- Good speakers prepare in advance for the kind of audience they speak to.
- A speaker is appreciated when he can create a rapport with the audience.
- Good speakers focus on the subject and do not go astray.
- One must keep within time and must stop when there is no more to say.

> **Think it over...**
>
> He who observes the speaker more than the sound of his words, will seldom meet with disappointments.
>
> — *J.K. Lavater*

Making Presentations

With advance in information technology it is now possible to make a variety of interesting presentations to different kinds of audience. Such presentations are now common in the corporate world to promote sales and train and motivate the personnel. With more people acquiring the skills to make useful presentations, their utilisation has grown in many fields. Some of the points that have emerged from the self-appraisal are:

- To be effective, a presentation must have a purpose.
- It is necessary to prepare in advance for a presentation.
- No presentation succeeds by itself. The speaker must co-relate the speech and the graphics.
- An interactive session after the presentation makes it more effective.
- The presentation must be concluded as soon as the purpose is achieved.

Communicating at Community Level

Everyone lives in a community. In everyday life one comes across many people who contribute towards our comfort and welfare by providing products and services of daily needs. To ignore these people, or to think that we can do without them, would be wrong. We are incomplete without them. These persons may have very small expectations from us, but these must be fulfilled if we want to get along well with them. Some of the points that have emerged from the self-appraisal are:

- Everyone needs to develop an attitude of gratitude. A simple "thank you" conveys that one is grateful for services rendered.
- An injury or fault is easily condoned when a person admits it by saying "sorry", which conveys that one is repentant.

- Lending a sympathetic ear helps others feel secure and comfortable.
- Those who are thoughtful of others will not be selfish or greedy.
- People must be accepted as they are, not as one would like them to be.

GETTING TO ACT

You have just gone through a variety of facts and observations on how effective communication touch different aspects of your life. Review them once again. Do it a little differently this time. Mark each statement with either a 'S' or a 'W'. If you feel that the statement describes a point of strength in your life, mark it 'S'. If you consider it a personal weakness, mark it 'W'. Now you have a list of both your strengths and weaknesses. Note them down separately on a piece of paper. While you would like to reinforce your strengths, it is also time to get over your weaknesses.

For each weakness, write what you can possibly do to get over it. Also note by when you can do it. This can be said to be setting a small goal. To achieve this goal, you will need to have a *Plan of Action*. This way, you will have a series of small goals that you want to attain, and also a series of *Plans of Action*. Can any of these be combined? If so, you can combine them. From amongst the list of goals, mark ones that are more important than the others. You might like to number them 1, 2, 3 and so on, number 1 representing the most important one. Allocate time to achieve each of the goals, one by one, over a set period.

A common fault by most people is that they keep these goals in their mind as activities they wish to undertake. This is not right. To be effective, the goals must be listed on paper. The *Plan of Action* too must also be worked out on paper for you to see, work on and sometimes review and redesign. Soon you will find that you are communicating effectively.

PLAN OF ACTION

Several issues will come before you, as you review the self-appraisal tests and plan action on each one of them. Combining some and acting on others independently, a grand plan will emerge before you. This is a plan you need to execute to develop habits that can become a part of your daily life, taking you towards more successful living. To ensure that the *Plan of Action* is balanced, you will do well to check the following:

- Will the plan help you to communicate more effectively?
- Will the plan help you to grow and develop your skills?
- Does the plan include time and activities for the family? For the spouse? And the children?
- Will you be more effective at the workplace?
- Does the plan have time for social activities? For the friends? For community service?
- Does the plan provide activities on daily, weekly and long-term basis?
- Does the plan provide a timeframe to achieve whatever is desired?

Once you know that there is a provision for everything, you can be sure that it is a balanced plan and you will benefit by it. Take special note of the timeframe and deadlines. Now you have a roadmap to become an effective communicator.

THE KEYWORD

'Action' is the keyword for attaining what you have set out to achieve. Go back to the earlier part describing how people communicate. You now know how you can communicate effectively. You have now to turn your thoughts to reality. You must earnestly desire to communicate effectively. Why? You want it because it will make you more effective at home, at the workplace and in the society. It will ultimately make you a better person. How? This will be possible through the positive, well-balanced *Plan of Action* that you have prepared.

Plans are only plans unless they are executed. To execute the plan, you will need to act; you will need to do what you have not been doing earlier. It will not be easy because it will require deliberate action that you are not used to. If you are convinced of the cause and committed to it, it will become easier. With each repeated activity, it will become simpler because it will pass on from the conscious mind to the subconscious and gradually become a habit.

Remind yourself of your school days and the discipline that was part of the school life. You did it for a long time. You carried it partially to your college life. Why did you let it slip by, for the sake of personal choice? When you bring the discipline back to everyday life, it will not only become easy but it will also add to your personal effectiveness.

> **Think it over...**
>
> A man who uses a great many words to express his meaning is like a bad marksman who, instead of aiming a single stone at an object, takes up a handful and throws at it in hopes he may hit it.
>
> – *Samuel Johnson*

POINTS TO PONDER

1. Periodic self-appraisal of personal skills helps a person to get over personal limitations.
2. Everyone is different. Do not try to be someone else.
3. Effective communication skills are based on good listening, speaking and writing skills.
4. Failing to be attentive, leads to poor communication skills.
5. Always seek the complete message. Confirm that you have understood it correctly.
6. Whenever in doubt, seek the answers from your conscience.
7. Believe in yourself. Keep reminding yourself that you can do it.
8. Learning is a continuous process. Only knowledge can dispel ignorance.
9. Confidence comes by developing an attractive personality.
10. Always remember God. When you need help, He will provide it.

11. Good reading skills lead to good speaking skills.
12. Good listening skills will lead to good conversational skills.
13. The telephone is a useful communication tool. Use it for your benefit.
14. Relationships in every sphere break down when communication becomes ineffective.
15. The ability to write good letters, memos and reports will make you a winner.
16. If you can communicate well, you will be able to handle good meetings.
17. Good speaking skills can be learnt through effort and perseverance.
18. It is as important to maintain good relationships in the community, as it is to maintain them within the home and workplace.
19. Review your strengths and weaknesses at least once every year.
20. Prepare a balanced Plan of Action to become an effective communicator.
21. The keyword to success is "action".

Communicating Effectively

Confidence comes from knowledge and experience. It is confidence that motivates a person to work harder and seek the support of others to be a "winner". At home, it makes the person more sensitive to the partner's feelings; at work, it differentiates between one who achieves and another who is easily satisfied. In the community, it makes a person stand out in the crowd.

Confidence emerges from the ability to communicate well at home, at the workplace, and in the community. The ability to communicate effectively is not a simple skill dependent upon a single activity. It comes from understanding and developing several faculties that involve observation, listening, speaking, writing and a positive attitude that is reflected in the body language.

With several faculties involved in the development of communication skills, it is a rare combination when a person can excel in all of them. It is a rare combination when a person can listen, speak and write well. Depending upon individual background and temperament some speak well, others write well. Some are able to develop their oratorical skills, others can express well only in writing.

In either case, a good all-round knowledge is important. Besides knowledge, it is the desire to be a "winner".

THINK SUCCESS

Everything begins with a thought. Through this thought a person visualises a dream, a dream to be a capable person, to be able to achieve great things. The dream creates a desire to turn the dream into a tangible reality. The desire motivates the person for action.

Think success. Visualise yourself as successful. Visualise yourself of acquiring good speaking and writing skills. Tell yourself that you are prepared to make the effort to turn your dreams into reality. Go through the self-appraisal exercises. Analyse your strengths and weaknesses. Prepare a *Plan of Action*. Set goals. Set deadlines. Act. Work towards success.

There are many obstacles on the path to success. Avoid people who discourage you from your goals. Avoid them even if they do it to caution you against pitfalls. Do not let small setbacks upset you. Do not panic. The world won't come to an end. Obstacles are a part of life. Problems come and go. Seek the friendship and support of good people. Seek the help of people who are knowledgeable, people who can guide and help you in your efforts. In turn, appreciate them. Be grateful for their support.

Resolve to communicate effectively in every sphere of life, be it at home, the workplace or the community. Observe etiquette and manners. Speak well on the phone, with your friends and colleagues. Write effective letters, memos and reports. Be known for your effective communication skills.

BECOME A GOOD LISTENER

To be an effective communicator, one must be a good listener. This requires a person to understand how the listening process works. The process of listening can be divided into smaller segments to understand it better.

- **Sensing** pertains to hearing the message.
- **Interpreting** refers to understanding what has been heard.
- **Evaluating** means forming an opinion of what has been said.
- **Remembering** refers to storage of the message for future use.
- **Responding** refers to acknowledging what has been said.

WHAT HINDERS LISTENING?

Several factors influence the listening process. Everyone must understand them.

- **Noise:** competes with what is being said.
- **Boredom:** is common when what is being said lacks attraction.
- **Mental block:** does not permit a person to accept a new idea.
- **Restlessness:** encourages interruptions by a person.
- **Fatigue:** takes away concentration to listen.

> **Think it over...**
>
> Precise knowledge is the only true knowledge, and he who does not teach exactly does not teach at all.
>
> — *Henry Ward Beacher*

LISTENING EFFECTIVELY

Listening effectively is an acquired skill. It requires one to concentrate on what is being said. It also requires one to refrain from speaking until the other person has finished conveying the message. Here are a few ways of becoming a good listener.

- Establish eye contact with the speaker. When you look at the speaker, there is an unsaid assurance that you are listening.
- Sit up with your back straight. That improves attentiveness.
- Think of how the information being provided will be useful to you.
- If extraneous thoughts invade your mind, remind yourself that what is being said is important to you.
- If it is a one-to-one session, confirm what has been conveyed to you by summing it up in your words.
- When you are part of a group to whom information is being imparted, nodding your head confirms that you are listening. If necessary, confirm the information at the end of the session.

- When the information is important, make notes immediately after the session. It will help make the information part of your memory.

THE READING HABIT

Most people are very poor readers. They are not even inclined to read the newspaper that they buy. The best they do is to look at the headlines on the front page, see if there are any interesting pictures and then put aside the newspaper. The younger people reach for the sports page. Most businessmen take a quick look at the business section, the stock exchange section and the advertisements. The family shares the Sunday newspaper. There is a little for everyone.

How many people subscribe to magazines? Very few, indeed! Some people read when they travel and have nothing to keep them occupied. Very few people are regular readers.

In how many homes do we see books? Most people will agree that they haven't bought a book since they left college. The book industry depends largely upon the textbook requirements in schools and colleges. The percentage of reading public is small.

All progress comes from the use of new knowledge. There can be no better way of passing knowledge than through books. Therefore, if one does not want to be left behind in life, one must read and read! There is no end to knowledge or to learning. The more you have of it, the more you want of it. Enjoy what you read. You will want more of it.

READING WITH A PURPOSE

Many of the people who read have strange choices. What do they read? Cheap magazines! When they read the newspaper, they will read about cases of theft, housebreaking or rape reported. When they read magazines, they are on the lookout for gossips and scandals about film and political personalities. Even the books they read pertain to scandals and murders. The circulation of these publications speaks of their popularity.

People who have goals to achieve cannot afford to read this kind of material. With limited time available, the reading has necessarily got to be purposeful. While reading, choose what appears important to you. A proper selection of reading material is essential. It is often quoted that you cannot judge a book by its cover. Do not be charmed by the cover. Read the blurb on the back cover. Check it with the contents. Browse through the book. If you find it will help you, buy the book.

ADJUSTING TO THE READING MATERIAL

All reading material does not deserve the same attention and time. Can a person read a newspaper word by word? If you were to try doing it, you would not complete it in a day. Again, can you read a magazine completely? How much time would it take? Do you have that much of time? It is just not practical. Only a limited time is available for this activity. One reads only as much as is possible.

Is it possible to read a textbook, as one would read a newspaper or a magazine? One could, but it would be of no use. A textbook, a book being read for leisure, a magazine and a newspaper would all require different kinds of reading attention. This makes it important that the reader must make adjustments with different kinds of reading material. Students need to read textbooks thoroughly. Magazines are read with the purpose of updating information. A newspaper is read to increase personal awareness about the activities in the community, the nation and around the world.

READING EFFICIENCY

Reading efficiency is reflected by the speed of one's reading. Most people feel that they read efficiently but it is not so. Experiments have repeatedly proved that the reading speed can be improved by at least 50 per cent. Increasing the speed is not enough. The comprehension of the subject must also be equally swift. Just think of the additional knowledge one can gain by improving reading efficiency. Excellent books on speed-reading are available in the market. The effort to improve reading efficiency will be amply repaid. As one learns to read faster, one also learns to comprehend the subject matter faster. Speed-reading is a positive step towards effective communication.

Think it over...

The three practical rules, then, which I have to offer are:

1. Never read any book that is not a year old.
2. Never read any book but the famed books.
3. Never read any book but what you like.

— *Ralph Waldo Emerson*

IMPROVING READING EFFICIENCY

To increase reading efficiency here are a few tips.

- Read as many books and magazines as you can.
- Be conscious of reading speed and assimilation.
- Have a wide eye span. Read several words at a time.
- Look for key words, phrases and ideas.
- Read in thought groups instead of reading words.
- Read mentally, not through spoken words. Lip movements reduce reading speed.
- Assimilate what the author writes. Do not confuse it with your opinions.
- Give the subject the importance it deserves.

EFFECTIVE CONVERSATION

An informal spoken interaction between two or more people is referred to as a conversation. This is a common form of communication between two or more people. While at home it may be the usual family exchanges pertaining to needs and exchange of views, at the workplace, conversation between managers, supervisors, workers, clients and customers carry forward the process of the business or profession. Much can be achieved or lost through effective or ineffective communication at this level. In the community, conversation helps procure personal needs and comforts and also offer personal services for the welfare of the community. To become a successful conversationalist:

- Talk less, listen more.
- Encourage the other person to talk.

- Ask questions to keep the conversation alive. The more the questions, the better the conversation. People provide a lot of information during a continued and tactful conversation.
- Ask open-ended questions beginning with who, what, when, why, where and how. They keep the conversation going. Conversation ends up with close-ended questions.
- The questions must highlight the positive aspects. Negative questions kill the conversation.
- Whenever a point is not clear, seek clarifications. The other person will provide them happily.
- To re-check information, repeat what you have understood. You could also re-word the statement or summarise to confirm it.
- Never interrupt the other person. This can break the chain of thoughts and you may not get the complete information.
- Keep encouraging the other person. This will confirm that you are taking interest in what the person has to say.

NEGOTIATING SKILLS

To negotiate means to reach an agreement through discussion. This is an everyday business activity particularly for those involved in selling. We see it everyday when housewives bargain the price of vegetables and other items in the marketplace. Negotiations at higher levels involve bulk sales or the sale of specialised items. Negotiations may also involve a variety of other situations and agreements, as we see teams from two countries negotiating boundary disputes or trade and barter agreements.

Negotiations involve two parties. Both desire to come to a mutual agreement. However, both the parties have their own benefits in mind. Each wants more advantage over the other. These situations require a high level of knowledge of the situation and excellent speaking and debating skills. To derive greater benefit each party would put forth objections. An effective negotiation would require that the person counter these objections with valid arguments through good speaking skills.

Objections based upon facts can be handled only by providing clarifications. The facts may have been misinterpreted. However, objections based upon emotional involvement are not easy to handle and require a high level of speaking skills. To negotiate successfully, the best path to follow is to verbally sell the advantages and benefits of coming to an agreement. These are difficult situations to handle, and one can succeed only through effort and perseverance.

SPEAKING IN PUBLIC

A step ahead of being an effective conversationalist is to possess the ability to speak in public. At the workplace, you may need to make presentations pertaining to your vocation. In the community, you may need to mould public opinion about a common cause. Although many do it in everyday life, only a few are good orators. To speak well in public:

- Be well informed. Unless you speak sense, no one would appreciate what you say. You must have a message to convey.

- Prepare well before speaking. Some of the people in the audience may know more than you about the subject.
- Remain composed when you stand up to speak. You will do well to take a few deep breaths before you begin speaking.
- Stand confidently at the podium. Learn to use the mike effectively. You should neither be too close to it, nor far away. Listen, as you speak. The sound must be balanced. Even as you look around at the audience while speaking, ensure that you maintain an equitable distance from the mike. Otherwise the effect would be lost.
- Modulate your voice in keeping with what you need to speak. A good speaker uses rhythm and tone to make the words touch the hearts of the audience.
- Keep within the time allocated to you. No organiser expects you to give a 30-minute speech in 10 minutes. In 10 minutes, give a 10-minute talk.
- Once you have completed what you have to say, stop speaking. Do not prolong the speech. You will be appreciated for it.

Think it over...

Courage, endurance, fearlessness and above all self-sacrifice are the qualities required of our leaders. A person exhibiting these qualities in their fullness would certainly be able to lead the nation; whereas the most finished orator, if he has not these qualities, must fail.

— *Mahatma Gandhi*

WRITING SKILLS

Everyone needs to write. The most elementary kind of writing one needs to do is to write letters. Have you ever thought of the many kinds of letters that you might need to write?

The commonest form of letters are those requesting for favours like seeking permission for leave from school, or to the municipal corporation for seeking a copy of a record. Then there are letters conveying gratitude for a favour or kindness shown. Besides the personal letters to friends and relatives, one may need to forward a complaint for lack of product quality or service. Sometimes you may need to extend invitations on birthdays or special occasions and also convey greetings on weddings, anniversaries or special days. Occasionally, you may need to write a letter of condolence.

At the workplace, there is always the need to communicate with the superiors through letters seeking leave or asking for favours and clarifications. Letters to suppliers, customers and clients are commonplace. At the community level, one needs to write to newspapers, clubs and other organisations. Sometimes it is necessary to seek donations and support from local philanthropists.

To make your letters effective, follow the simple rules discussed earlier. Use the language the other person can understand. Ensure that the letter is clear, concise, courteous, convincing and complete. Use a good letterhead; write it legibly and neatly. Let it bear the stamp of your personality. It is your personal messenger. When you receive a letter, respond to it at the earliest. You will be appreciated for it.

FINDING AN EASY WAY

Most people are too lazy to write or respond to letters. This is a human weakness. If you need to get ahead in life, you will have to get over this habit. Even if you communicate by writing two lines on a postcard it would be appreciated. Till you transform your habit there is an easy way out.

A variety of cards conveying different kinds of messages are available in the market. Greeting cards sent on special occasions like Diwali, Christmas, Eid, Raksha Bandhan, Bhaiya Dooj and other festivals are popular. However, the market is also flooded with "thank you" cards, "get well" cards, or cards conveying greetings on getting promotions, passing an examination or being honoured. Keep these handy. Write your name and send them. They will communicate your feelings and goodwill. Your gesture will be appreciated.

WRITING SKILLS AT THE WORKPLACE

Innumerable written notes, memos, letters, and reports exchange hands at the workplace everyday. Each of these communications is important. If it were not so, there would have been no need to write one. The effectiveness of each of these communications depends upon how well it is written, read and comprehended.

To be effective, all kinds of communication are time bound. A certain amount of importance and urgency makes it necessary that the message reaches the right place at the right time. In this regard reports are most urgent. Many need to be filled in every day, some weekly and others on completion of parts of the assignment. When reporting stops, the progress of the work stops. Memos and letters are next on the priority list. One cannot afford not to act upon them. They must be attended to according to their importance.

Detailed reports pertaining to achievements, ongoing projects or future plans and potential are documents that need good writing skills, which only a few persons possess at any workplace. These are important documents used by the management to evaluate progress and to plan for the future. Factual information is important. These reports need to be correctly structured and written. Once written, the report will require revision and editing. Since much of the information will be in the form of cold, hard facts, making the report reader friendly is an art only a few possess.

Written communication will continue to play an important role at the workplace. To be effective, there is only one way. Master the language. Write and re-write. Learn from your own successes and failures. Practise paves the way to success.

Think it over...

The strokes of the pen need deliberation, as much as those of the sword need swiftness.

— *Julia Ward Howe*

WRITING A NEWS RELEASE

Good public relations help promote a good cause. This may necessitate the issue of a news release to the press for inclusion in the next day's newspaper.

News is what actually happens. What people say or do is news. It is important that the reporting must be accurate and complete. The language must be clear so that it may not be misinterpreted.

The news release must draw immediate attention. It must be brief. Have an eye-catching heading. It should be short, but must convey what the write-up is all about. The opening sentence should describe the important aspects of the news story. The sentences that follow should elaborate upon the news story. This way the reader gets to know the story thrice. First, from the heading; second, from the opening sentence and third from the sentences that elaborate the story. This makes the news release effective.

TELEPHONE ETIQUETTE

With a revolution in telecommunications, almost everyone has an access to a telephone or mobile. It is a great communication tool, but one must understand how it works and how it must be used. Every telephone has a number. The first part refers to the number of the telephone exchange and the rest to the use. For example, if your number is 2732 5016, the exchange number is 2732 and your number is 5016. Every city has a number too. For example, Delhi is 011, Mumbai is 022, Kolkata is 033 and Chennai is 044. The country is also identified with a number. India is identified with the number 91.

It is not possible to remember all the numbers one needs to contact. Therefore, one must keep a directory of the numbers. For emergency use, the numbers of the hospital, fire brigade, railways, the bus terminal, police station and the family doctor must be listed on the first page.

Remember these simple ideas to communicate on the telephone:

- Ensure that you dial the correct number. On getting connected, disclose your identity and ask for the person you wish to talk to. If it is a business call and the person is not available, leave your contact details with the receptionist or the telephone operator.
- If you get the wrong number, say "sorry" and hang up.
- If you are connected to a computerised exchange, follow the instructions that are conveyed to you. Most airports and railway stations have computerised response centres.
- When you speak on the phone, it is your voice that makes or mars your image. Smile, as you speak courteously. Be polite. Do not use improper language. Do not simultaneously speak on the phone and also converse with a person sitting beside you. This can be misleading.
- In many cities where home service facilities are offered, when you give your contact details, also give directions and landmarks to reach your address quickly.
- When dialing international numbers, please check the time of the country where you are calling. It may be daytime at your location, but it could be midnight in the country where you have called.
- Receptionists who receive all business calls and direct them to appropriate persons need to be careful about voice training. Their jobs depend upon it.

- At all times be polite and courteous on the telephone. Your image will linger in the minds of the people you talk to.

MOBILE PHONE ETIQUETTE

A mobile phone is very much like a normal phone, but considering its size, it can be carried anywhere. Therefore, besides the normal courtesies required in using a telephone, it is necessary to observe a few additional precautions.

- In the normal course use the landline number only. Use the mobile number only when you need to reach a person directly.
- Just because you have a person's mobile number, it does not mean that you can reach him or her any time. Do not ring at odd hours. If it is an emergency, apologize for the interruption and explain why you needed to call.
- Even in the normal routine when you ring a mobile number, ask if you are not interrupting the person at his work or that he is not driving or in a place where he is unable to respond to the call.
- Switch off the mobile or the ringer, when you are in a meeting. It is commonplace to hear mobile phones ringing at odd times and places.
- Do not use the mobile phone when driving. It could cause a serious accident.
- Keep the mobile phone away when fuelling your scooter or car.

AVOID OFFENSIVE COMMUNICATION

Even knowledgeable persons cause offence through habits that reflect lack of understanding for others' feelings. People adorn homes with fancy table and wall clocks. Men and women wear watches to match their lifestyle. Children are not far behind. They too have a fancy variety to show off at school. What is the purpose? Watches are intended to tell time. One would imagine everyone is very time conscious. But is it so? Punctuality means little to many of us. Let us learn to respect each other's time.

The civic authorities provide dustbins to throw trash. Do we use them? It is far easier to throw trash across the street or along the neighbour's boundary wall. Spittoons have been provided at many places. Ask any person fond of *paan*. He is thrilled to spit on the wall or on the road.

The doormat comes in all shapes and varieties. It waits patiently for people to clean the underside of the shoes. But no, why waste time? A little mud will not hurt the floor. The floor has to be mopped in the morning anyway. Smoking is injurious to health. Ask the non-smokers, who are compelled to inhale the smoke. Ask the poor carpet or the bed linen. They bear the burns and the ashes. Even the poor ashtrays lie ignored. Nobody likes to use them.

The poor soap dish, the hand towels and taps are in no less trouble. The soap dish is ignored. The soap lies soggy. The towels are messy. The taps are running. So what if there is water shortage? Can't a person be comfortable in his own home? Why spare crockery from misuse? It is slowly moved from the dining area to the television viewing area and even to the rooms. Look at the brighter side. It gives the housewife some additional exercise in getting it back where it belongs.

Everyone loves music. Why should the neighbourhood not know that you have a 1000-watt system? So what if there are elderly and sick people? If they find it disturbing, it is their business. After all, you are playing the music system in your home. The next time you organise a *Jagrata* or a birthday party, get the loudest DJ in town. These functions are not celebrated everyday. If the system is not loud enough, how will the neighbourhood know about the celebrations?

People build walls around their homes to keep intruders out. These provide an excellent place to stick posters of all descriptions. Big walls provide a nice place to paint messages on. Even the direction boards, the "No Parking" boards or even private boards provide an ideal place to paste the smaller posters.

Each day, many of us try the patience of family members, friends and neighbours by doing things that can be avoided. Can we do without the goodwill of others? Why do we act helpless to disturb and offend others? A little thoughtfulness on our part can make the community a happier place to live in. Etiquette and good manners communicate thoughtfulness and goodwill.

Think it over...

Manners are of more importance than law. Upon them, in a great measure, the law depends. The law touches us but here and there, or now or then. Manners are what vex or soothe, corrupt or verify, exalt or debase, barbarise or refine us, by a constant, steady, uniform, insensible operation, like that of the air we breathe.

— *Edmund Burke*

COMMUNICATION ON SPECIAL OCCASIONS

Nobody's life is a smooth ride. There will be difficult occasions. Not everyone takes these problems in the normal stride. Many buckle under pressure. Some seek support. A few go through accepting them as a part of life.

People visit hospitals for two reasons – as a patient requiring medical attention, or to visit a friend or relative in hospital. Do not be a difficult patient. Do not forget that you are one amongst many. You may need special attention, but so do other patients. The doctors and the nurses have to look after the needs of everyone. When you observe patience, you will get better attention.

As a visitor, go to a hospital only during visiting hours. If you are suffering from a cold, cough or fever, avoid visiting the hospital. You may communicate infection to the patient. Do not take children to the hospital. They are at risk of catching an infection. Many of them create a ruckus running up and down the corridors disturbing the patients. Maintain silence within the hospital. Do not talk too much to the patient or suggest any medication to get well soon. Keep your visit as short as possible.

When invited by friends, you may need to visit religious ceremonies in a temple, mosque, a church or a gurudwara. Customs vary from one community to another. Through ignorance you are at a risk to hurt religious sentiments if you are not acquainted with the customs. It is advisable that you must check on these and follow what is suggested to you. For example, you need to take off shoes in temples, wear a scull cap in mosques and have your head covered in a gurudwara.

Visiting a home where someone has died often poses communication challenges. Do not overlook that the members of the immediate family are bereaved. It is not easy to get over a long association with the deceased person. The grief can take its toll. Be patient. It is not necessary to express the condolence verbally. Your presence in itself is an acknowledgement of your concern and sympathy.

Even in normal circumstances one needs to be cautious when visiting public places like public toilets, parks, bus terminals, railway stations and other utilities. One is free to use them, but not deface them. It is everyone's responsibility to keep public places clean. One must leave them in a state that is right for others to use after you.

Hotels and restaurants are semi-public places. They are not entirely free from misuse by persons unaware of others' convenience. Etiquette and good manners make life smooth for everyone. For a happy journey through life get acquainted with local customs and traditions. Even at the workplace get to know the established norms of working. You must appreciate that you do not communicate only through the spoken and the written word, but are rather communicating all the time through your activities. Your actions, both good and bad, add on to project your image in the society.

POINTS TO PONDER

1. Confidence emerges from the ability to communicate well in the home, the workplace and the community.
2. Think success. Visualise yourself as successful.
3. Effective communication skills are based upon good listening skills.
4. Everyone needs to be a good conversationalist.

5. Good conversational skills lead to good negotiation skills.
6. Few become orators. The vast majority can learn to speak effectively in public.
7. Writing skills are as important as speaking skills.
8. When short of time, communicate effectively through ready-made cards.
9. Written communication predominates at the workplace. It helps you become a "winner".
10. The telephone must be used effectively.
11. One can generate a lot of ill will through bad habits and behaviour.
12. Everyone needs to face a variety of situations in life. Face them with confidence.